"*The Money Challenge* by Art Rainer is an excellent book on how to be financially responsible. The three-fold challenge to give generously, save wisely, and live appropriately is mapped out in clear, practical, and obtainable steps. God designed us to be generous and wise with our resources. This short and easy-to-read work will help you get there. I am delighted to commend it to you."

Daniel L. Akin, president, Southeastern Baptist
Theological Seminary, Wake Forest, North Carolina

"Art has written an incredibly practical, readable, useful book on living openhandedly with our finances. *The Money Challenge* offers practical steps to live as God has designed us to: as channels of His great generosity, to advance His Kingdom. I highly recommend it!"

Matt Carter, pastor of preaching and vision,
The Austin Stone Community Church, Austin, Texas

"I can't wait for you to read Art's book. It is so good. Art encourages and equips you in *The Money Challenge*. Not only will you learn a lot, but you will also enjoy his captivating writing style."

Derwin L. Gray, lead pastor, Transformation Church,
Indian Land, South Carolina

"Sometimes the hardest part of wise financial stewardship is knowing where to start. That's where Art's book comes in—his relatable stories and practical steps break down a seemingly impossible goal to simple, faith-filled steps. Join him in this thirty-day challenge and watch as God uses this book to propel you into a lifestyle of generous giving. Around The Summit Church we always say, 'Live sufficiently, give extravagantly.' This is how to start."

J.D. Greear, PhD, pastor of The Summit Church,
Raleigh-Durham, North Carolina, and author, *Gaining by Losing:
Why the Future Belongs to Churches that Send*

"*The Money Challenge* is a hopeful, gospel-oriented primer on using finances for the sake of the Kingdom. Everyone can benefit from the biblical wisdom here, regardless of financial or social background."

Russell Moore, president, Southern Baptist
Ethics & Religious Liberty Commission

"Who knew generosity was such a driving force for how we handle our money in a God-honoring way? Art Rainer helps us understand why in this helpful book, *The Money Challenge*. If we're honest, money is one of the hardest topics for us to face and tackle in our hearts and minds. That is one of many reasons we are served by Rainer's work here. Practical, wise, and challenging, you'll be glad you picked up this helpful book."

Trillia Newbell, author of *Enjoy, Fear and Faith,* and *United*

"Pastors and church leaders: run to this book! I wish I had this book when I was a pastor. It is short, easy to read, and filled with practical steps to lead a congregation toward greater biblical stewardship. I would give a copy to everyone in my church. Those who take these steps will have a church filled with joyous givers!"

Thom S. Rainer, president and CEO, LifeWay Christian Resources

"People have written at length about how to live debt-free or save for retirement, but few have written about the reason for doing these things. Why should you work to become debt-free? Why should you save for retirement? In *The Money Challenge*, Art Rainer gives clear, biblically based, practical wisdom about why we should give generously, save wisely, and live appropriately.

"The thirty money challenges are opportunities for you to put into practice what you have learned. They are simple yet valuable steps to help you become a better steward of God's resources."

Jimmy Scroggins, senior pastor of Family Church,
West Palm Beach, Florida

"Have you ever found yourself waking up from your financial dreams, recognizing your reality is quite different? *The Money Challenge* creatively teaches and enables you to honor God through your life and finances. Thanks, Art, for tackling this tough topic."

Dave Stone, pastor, Southeast Christian Church,
Louisville, Kentucky

THE
MONEY
CHALLENGE

978-1-4336-5030-7

Published by B&H Publishing Group
Nashville, Tennessee

Dewey Decimal Classification: 332.024
Subject Heading: STEWARDSHIP \
PERSONAL FINANCE \ MONEY

1 2 3 4 5 6 • 21 20 19 18 17

THE
MONEY
CHALLENGE

30 DAYS OF DISCOVERING GOD'S DESIGN
FOR YOU AND YOUR MONEY

ART RAINER

PUBLISHING GROUP

NASHVILLE, TENNESSEE

To my three sons:
Nathaniel
Joshua
James

Every morning and every night, I tell you three things:
I love you.
I am proud of you.
And I am glad that you are my sons.

I pray that you will never forget it.

Acknowledgments

Though only one name is on the front cover of this book, it took a team to pull it off. To everyone who assisted me in this process, thank you.

I love my family. They are such a great source of encouragement and inspiration for me. Our three boys, Nathaniel, Joshua, and James—you fill our house with life, laughter, and several dents in the walls. I could not be more proud to be your dad. Sarah, somehow you are able to work within the chaos that comes with a house full of boys. You are a good wife and mom.

Of course, the rest of my family deserves mentioning as well, starting with my parents, Thom and Nellie Jo Rainer. Thank you for giving me a childhood home that feared and loved God. And for the rest of the crew—Sam, Jess, Erin, Rachel, Tom, Dale, Stephanie, David, Canon, Harper, Will, Collins, Maggie, Bren, Joel, Kaitlyn, and Connor—I love you all too.

I am thankful to B&H for giving me this opportunity. It is truly a great honor to partner with such an outstanding team. Devin Maddox, I appreciate your work. You are an excellent editor. Thank you for your consistent enthusiasm and encouragement about this book.

One of the great blessings in my life is to serve alongside so many amazing people at Southeastern Baptist Theological Seminary in Wake Forest, North Carolina. I am grateful to the faculty, staff, and students for their persistent passion for the Great Commission. Specifically, I want to thank Amy Whitfield, our director of communications. Your input made this book better.

Finally, I am thankful for my Lord and Savior Jesus Christ. My desire is that this book will be used to advance His Kingdom by helping believers discover God's design for them and their money. May we become people who are known not to be hoarders, but conduits through which His generosity flows.

Contents

GENEROSITY KILLERS

There Is Something More

As Annie walked down Chicago's Michigan Avenue, she struggled to suppress the desire to walk into every single high-end clothier and try on a few outfits. They called this stretch of retail and restaurant paradise the "Magnificent Mile." Annie agreed. It was magnificent.

While pausing to look at a perfectly showcased outfit displayed through a store window, her phone vibrated.

She looked at her phone. She had a new, unread e-mail from her wireless phone provider. Annie quickly put the phone back into her pocket. She didn't want to read the e-mail. She didn't need to.

Annie let out a frustrated sigh.

It was another past-due notice. She had missed another bill. And just like the other times, she found herself somewhat angry, somewhat embarrassed, and totally frustrated.

"Why do I even care anymore?" she muttered to herself as she slightly shook her head.

Never would she have imagined that this would be her—the woman who could not pay her bills. Two years ago when Annie received her college diploma, it seemed as if the entire world was there for the taking. She had dreams. She was going to make a difference in people's lives.

She was destined for significance.

She was launching into one great big adventure.

Instead, she found herself in a free fall, getting swallowed up by the world she thought she would change.

It started when Annie didn't get hired for her dream job. They took another applicant from her school. Somehow that person was more qualified, or at least that's what she was told. So she took another less paying, less glamorous job. She figured she needed something to pay her food, rent, utilities, and car lease—just something to get her by until she found another job.

It worked, for about a month.

Annie quickly realized that she needed more money. Her college years had caught up to her. Education was not cheap, and she had accumulated a mountain of student loan debt. And, unfortunately, she never lived like a college student. As a college freshman, she received a number of credit card offers and she accepted most of them. Over the next few years, Annie racked up a significant amount of credit card debt. To put the cherry on top of her financial mess, she was at the end of her car lease and had put way too many miles on her vehicle. She was going to owe the dealership a lot of money, and there was no way she could purchase the car.

Now she really regretted always volunteering to drive and taking spontaneous road trips with her friends. Who knows how many miles she had put on the car without even thinking?

Just as Annie started walking again, a voice called out to her.

"Excuse me, ma'am. Do you have any change?"

He was an elderly, homeless man. The wrinkles on his face and the pain in his walk communicated a life of struggle.

Annie's heart went out to him, and she started walking toward him.

"What is your name?" Annie gently questioned.

"Randall."

"Nice to meet you, Randall. My name is Annie."

Annie reached in her purse and pulled out her wallet. But as she opened her wallet, what she didn't see broke her heart.

There was nothing. No dollars, no change. Instead, she found an old receipt from a nice restaurant two blocks from where she stood. It was another reminder of the many bad decisions she had made.

She stood there looking at the empty wallet and began to cry. What had she done? She couldn't even help an elderly, homeless man.

"I'm sorry, Randall. I want to, but I really have nothing to give you."

Randall released a big, kind grin, showcasing three missing teeth.

"Don't worry about it, Ms. Annie. I can see your heart. You have a great day."

"I'm sorry," she tearfully whispered.

And with that Annie turned from Randall, tears still running down her cheeks.

———

Charles forcefully pushed open the glass doors that led out of the busy office tower. As he stepped onto the sidewalk outside, he was immediately hit with a hair-rustling cool breeze and the sound of cars honking their horns. Several straight-faced people briskly walked past him. Clearly, they had places to be. They always did. Downtown was consistently hectic, which is why Charles fit in so well.

As he turned to walk down the sidewalk, his phone vibrated.

He pulled the phone out of his pocket and looked at the caller identification. It was his wife. This was the second time she had called today. But just like the first time, he didn't have time to talk to her. He was hurrying to an important meeting. Charles declined the call and put the phone back in his pocket.

Charles was a very successful businessperson. He had worked his way up the corporate ladder for the past twenty years. He was now a top-level advertising executive working with some of his company's biggest clients, like the one he was on his way to see now.

Of course, there was a price for his success. There was little time for family or anything else. He was always on call. If his clients needed him, he was there. Sure, there were times when his priorities were off a little bit. On the morning of his son's eighth birthday, he received a call from a client. They wanted to start working on an advertising campaign immediately. Charles told his wife and his son he would be back that afternoon for the party. But his son blew out the candles without him there.

Charles justified the time away from family as taking care of them financially, making sure they had a good life. In the back of his mind, he knew they didn't need all the money he made, but that justification helped cover up the reality that he was addicted to money and possessions.

Charles began to move quickly on the sidewalk, but a couple of gazing Chicago tourists got in his way. They seemed not to notice that Charles was behind them.

"People have to work here," he said in a heated but quiet voice.

He was close enough to the tourists that they could hear him. They started to move to the side, but it wasn't quick enough for Charles. He bolted to the left of them, accidently running into a young woman who never saw him coming through the tears running down her face.

Just then, a man on the side of the street called out to Charles, "Sir, you don't happen to have any change, do you?"

"Are you serious?" replied Charles, who was clearly frustrated.

"I'd appreciate any amount."

"You know what I'd appreciate? I'd appreciate it if you went and got a job. I'd appreciate you not loitering around this sidewalk. I'd appreciate it if you would leave me alone instead of asking me for money every day. Yes, I do have a wallet full of money. Unlike you, I don't have to ask anybody for anything, because I work for it. And no, you can't have any. Stop asking me! Now go get a job, Randall!"

Charles hurried off.

He hated being late.

———

Annie stood there in shock. The man had practically run her over. There was no "sorry" or "excuse me." It was as if she were invisible. Annie looked down and saw her phone. Apparently, it had fallen out of her purse when the man hit her. She squatted down to pick it up. The screen was cracked.

"Great."

Annie looked up, and through her tears, she could see Randall. She felt bad for him. Then she thought about the man who hit her.

How could a man with a wallet full of money be so unhappy? He had everything she did not, and probably a phone that was not cracked. Yet, he was miserable.

"If I ever get out of this financial mess, I will be different," she promised to herself.

She went over to Randall.

"Randall, I don't know when, but I will be back to help you. I want to make a difference with my life. Better yet, I want to make a difference in your life."

She gave Randall a hug. Randall hugged back.

"I know you will, Ms. Annie. I know you will."

There was that great smile of his again.

———

Many of us find ourselves like Annie. We want to do more and be more. We want to make a difference in this world. We want our lives to count for something significant. But our finances are wrecked, sometimes caused by our own doing and sometimes caused by things completely out of our control. We need to clean up the financial mess, but we don't want to do it just so we can be rich.

We've seen men and women like Charles. Perhaps we are like Charles ourselves. While they seem to have everything, they have nothing. They are miserable. We want nothing to do with that.

Being rich is not the answer. Financial health is not even the final answer. There is something more. Financial health is not itself an end, but a means to a much more significant and fulfilling end.

Friends, welcome to *The Money Challenge*.

CHAPTER 1

Do You Accept the Challenge?

The next day, Annie walked into the local bank. She could not remember the last time she had been there. But she knew that she had to start somewhere, and a bank seemed as good a place as any.

"Is there anything I can do for you?" asked an approaching man.

Annie sighed.

"I don't know. I'm pretty much a financial train wreck and just need to talk to somebody about how to fix it."

"Ah. Well, you are at the right bank. You need to talk to G.B." With a folded piece of paper in his hand, he pointed to a man sitting behind a desk.

"G.B.?"

"I believe it actually stands for George Bailey, but everyone likes to say that it stands for Generous Banker."

"Okay. That's kind of weird."

"Trust me. You'll like him. I just finished meeting with him."

Annie figured that she didn't have anything to lose at this point so she followed the man to G.B.'s desk.

"G.B., this lady needs to meet with you," the man said as he motioned Annie to sit down in front of his desk. "Thank you, Terry!" the man behind the desk said with a big, comforting grin. As Terry left, G.B.'s attention turned toward Annie.

"My name is G.B. How can I help you?"

"I know. I mean, that guy, Terry, told me your name. My name is Annie, and," she paused, "my finances are a total disaster. Actually. I feel like my life is a total disaster."

Annie didn't expect to unload all her problems on the banker. After all, she had just met him. But she told him about everything. Her bad decision-making. Her debt. Her bills. Everything. She even told him about Randall. At the end of it, tears were slowly trickling down her cheeks.

"I just feel like God has made me for something more. And I can't shake the sense that, somehow, the way I use money is holding me back. I want to make a difference, but I can't. I'm stuck."

G.B. handed her a tissue. He then began to write on a small notepad.

"You are made for something more. Your money was made for something more. Look, God's formula for money is simple: Give generously, save wisely, and live appropriately. You will find the 'more' you are seeking in His design."

He ripped the page out of the notepad, folded the paper, and handed it to Annie.

"Here is what we are going to do. I want you to stop by every few days. We don't have to meet long, but each time I want to tell you a part of God's design for you and your money. And each time I will give you a couple of Money Challenges."

"Money Challenges?" Annie questioned. Her face went from sad to inquisitive.

"That's right, Money Challenges. Your first two are on that paper. I look forward to seeing you in a few days." He was smiling.

"Um, okay? I'll see you in a few days, I guess." She was not confident in her answer.

Annie got up and walked out the door, unsure if she would actually return. But then again, what other hope did she have?

And she was curious about what made this guy the "Generous Banker."

———

What's Going On Here?

What you do with your money matters. Just ask Elisabeth Dunn. She knows.

Elisabeth Dunn is a researcher interested in the relationship between money and happiness. She has spent years exploring it. Dunn and her colleagues have performed several studies trying to figure out if and when money increases happiness. The results are worth noting. Let's take a quick glance at two of the studies.

Study #1: Toddlers and Generosity[1]

On one side of the table stands the toddler. On the other side of the table sits the brown monkey puppet, creatively named Monkey, with its "handler." Both the child and Monkey have a single, small bowl in front of them on the table. A woman in the room points out a fact that would depress any toddler: "Both you and Monkey have no treats right now."

The child notices the absence of treats. The woman in the room is correct. There are no treats.

The woman in the room suddenly "finds" eight Goldfish crackers and places them in the toddler's bowl. Shortly after, the woman in the room "finds" another Goldfish cracker and gives it to Monkey. The puppet acts like it is eating the treat. Next, the woman in the room "finds" another treat for Monkey, but this time she hands it to the toddler. She asks the toddler to give it to Monkey, and the toddler does. Monkey eats that treat as well. Finally, the woman in the room asks the toddler to give one of their Goldfish crackers to the Monkey, a sacrificial act.

And the toddler does.

Researchers repeated the same experiment with twenty-two toddlers and recorded their level of enthusiasm during each step. The results were fascinating. Toddlers exhibited the *greatest* enthusiasm when they gave one of their *own* treats to Monkey. This was that final, sacrificial act.

They experienced the greatest happiness when they gave away what was in their possession. Monkey was happy, and they were too.

Study #2: Adults and Generosity[2]

In another experiment, adults rated their happiness level in the morning. They were then handed an envelope containing either $5 or $20. The recipients of the envelopes were given one of two instructions for the day—instructions to spend the money on themselves or instructions to spend it on others. Each of the adults did as they were instructed. Later that evening, the envelope recipients were given a call and asked, once again, to rate their happiness level. The result? Those who spent their money on others were happier than those who spent it on themselves.

Elisabeth Dunn's studies are telling us something.

But what?

It's Not Working

In the beginning, God created everything. He created the blue sky, the green grass, the yellow sun, and the black depths of the oceans. He created all the fish of the sea, the birds of the air, and the creatures that roam the dry land. He created man, and He created woman. And for a time, everything was good.

Why was it good?

It was good because everything operated as it should. All plants, animals, weather patterns, and humans had a very specific God-given design, and they were all functioning according to that design.

But then, sin entered the world. This sin threw off everything. Everything was no longer good. Adam and Eve decided to try something outside of God's original design, believing the lie of the Serpent. It left them broken, hurt, and unsatisfied.

So this is where we are—humans living in an imperfect world, often trying to operate in a way that goes against our original design. We try to figure out marriage apart from God. We try to figure out parenting apart from God. And we try to figure out money apart from God. Yet, we still find ourselves broken, hurt, and unsatisfied. What we thought would provide fulfillment leaves us empty.

Maybe you have had these thoughts before:

"If I could only get that raise, then I'd be happy."

"If I could only pay off that debt, then I would be free and could find satisfaction."

"If I could only buy that house and get that car."

But then you get that raise.

You pay off that debt.

You buy that house and you get that car.

But it didn't work. It didn't have the effect you thought it would. You found that the happiness you acquired was only momentary. Like the adults in Dunn's study, you are better off financially, but you aren't as happy as you should be.

Something is missing.

Something is wrong.

When Something Went Right

Late one afternoon, my wife, Sarah, came to me. With her phone in her hand, I could tell she had been texting. Her hesitant expression told me that she was about to either tell or ask me something that was out of the norm.

"I've been texting back and forth with Amy."

Amy and her husband, Larry, were good friends of ours from Florida.

She continued, "They're struggling financially. Larry hasn't been making very much at his job. They are a few months behind on their rent and other bills. And Christmas is coming up. They have no idea how they will be able to purchase any gifts for their two kids."

Larry was a hard worker, but he held a commission-only job that sometimes brought on lean times for the family. I had seen them struggle before but not like this. I could not stand the thought of them being in this situation. I hurt for them. And I hated imagining their kids not having anything for Christmas.

"Can we help?" Sarah asked.

"How much are you thinking?"

"$1,000 for the bills and a $200 toy store gift card for the kids' Christmas."

That was a lot of money. Of course, I knew they could use it. They could actually use more. Fortunately, we had managed our money pretty well thus far in our marriage. And more importantly, I felt God tugging on my heart. We needed to do this.

"Sure. I'll pick up the gift card in the morning," I said.

Sarah smiled. I did too. I was glad we could help.

That decision brought about happiness and a satisfaction that I have found to be rare when it relates to money. I like my coffee-maker. I'm glad I bought it. I like my car. I'm glad I bought it too.

But the thought of those purchases does not produce the same feeling I get when I think about using our money to help our friends in need, to give to something outside of ourselves.

So what does that tell me about money? And what can Dunn's research teach us about money? It's the same thing the Bible teaches us. You and your money are designed for something much bigger than wealth accumulation.

We are wired to use our money for something far more significant than ourselves. God has designed us (and any resources we have) to make a difference in this world.

Many people work extremely hard to manage their finances so that they can spend their money on whatever they want. They are "free." But when was the last time a financial decision conjured up feelings of rich satisfaction? When was the last time the way you handled your money provided deep, refreshing happiness?

It probably occurred when you weren't hoarding riches, but were giving them away.

Something More

I used to get the story of the widow's gift wrong. Though I knew the narrative well, my imagination gave me an incorrect image of this woman. In this story, we find Jesus sitting near the temple treasury. This is where people would stop by and drop off their offerings to God. Jesus watched as the rich dropped large amounts of money into the treasury. Certainly, God must be happy with them.

Then, Jesus watched as a poor widow came by and placed two small coins in the treasury. The Bible tells us that these coins were worth very little. As Jesus witnessed this event, He called His disciples over.

> *"Truly I tell you," he said. "This poor widow has put in more than all of them. For all these people have put in gifts out of their surplus, but she out of her poverty."* (Luke 21:3–4)

So what did I get wrong? You see, I grew up in the days of Sunday school flannel graphs. (These were flannel-covered boards on which flannel character cutouts were placed to teach a Bible story.) I know some of you can relate. Inevitably, when the story of the widow's gift was told, on the board was placed a flannel lady who looked incredibly sad. She was old, hunched over, and sad. It was as if the gift she gave was an act of misery for her. I always felt bad for that flannel lady. So whenever I would read the story of the widow, I would experience a sense of pity toward her.

But 2 Corinthians 9:7 says this: *"Each person should do as he has decided in his heart—not reluctantly or out of compulsion, since God loves a cheerful giver."*

So why would Jesus use a person who gave out of misery to illustrate giving? This is where I got it all wrong. I let the flannel graph widow influence my imagination too much. It was more likely that this woman was not grimacing but smiling, cheek to cheek. When you were around her, you probably did not sense burden. In fact, I bet she was one of the most joyful individuals in that temple area.

God designed us to be generous. And He designed us to be generous in ways that expand His Kingdom. God designed us not to be hoarders but to be conduits through which His generosity flows.

When we are generous, we get closer to God's original design for how we should operate. And when we get closer to God's original design for how we should operate, we will find ourselves more happy, satisfied, and full of purpose with not just our money, but our entire lives. Elisabeth Dunn's research tells us this. And more importantly, God tells us this.

Why do we need to manage our money well?

So that we can live with our hands wide open, ready to be generous when God calls us to do so. When we operate as God designed, by giving to advance His Kingdom, we will find greater purpose and happiness in our money.

Finding God's Design for You and Your Money

This is not just a book to help you manage your finances well for the sake of having well-managed finances. This is not just a book to help you think through debt elimination and retirement for the sake of debt elimination and retirement.

We will discuss those things because they are important, but they are not the ultimate goals. We discuss them because they are part of a much larger, more adventurous, and more satisfying goal. They are not an end, but a means to an end. *I am not nearly as concerned about you being rich as I am you being enriched.*

God has designed us to manage and use money in a particular way. When we align our decision-making with His design, we will find ourselves using our money for an adventure that we could never orchestrate.

Let's start looking at how we are going to get there.

Your Three-Step Formula

Sometimes, we make money too complex. We hear financial recommendations that are beyond our understanding, so we tune out. We assume that those who manage their money well are simply smarter than we are in this area, and we are doomed to a life of poor financial choices. But it doesn't have to be that way.

Over the next few chapters, we will walk through a three-step formula that can be derived from the Bible. It is not original to me—many great leaders use and teach this formula. And it is not complex, because managing our money does not have to be.

What is this three-step formula?

1. *Give generously.*
2. *Save wisely.*
3. *Live appropriately.*

It's that simple.

As you read this book, you will uncover what it means to give generously, save wisely, and live appropriately. You will also find a few financial guidelines. The purpose of these guidelines is not only to get you financially healthy, but also to help you experience the adventure-filled, others-focused, generous life that God designed you to live.

Do You Accept the Challenge?

Who says you have to get all your finances in order before you can start developing a lifestyle of generosity? Certainly, getting financially healthy will launch you into a level of generosity that you have never been able to experience. But why not develop the pattern of generosity as you work on your financial picture? Why not start the adventure on which God designed you to be today?

At the end of each chapter, you will find the Money Challenges Annie receives.

But they aren't just for Annie. They are your Money Challenges as well.

Some require money; some do not. All challenge you to develop a lifestyle of generosity, a life that lives for something much larger than yourself. Are you ready to align yourself with God's plan for your money? Are you ready to put yourself on the path of open-handed, Kingdom-minded, generous living?

Do you accept the challenge?

If so, let's get started.

————

Annie looked down at the paper and saw the first challenges:

Day 1 Money Challenge: *Spend time in prayer.* Pray that God will give you the courage to have the discussions that need to take place and to make the decisions that need to be made. Pray that God will show you where you can be generous.

Day 2 Money Challenge: *Consider what generosity has meant to you.* We have all been the recipients of another's generosity. Take a moment to consider what it meant to you to be the recipient of that generosity. Answer these questions: Who gave? What did they give? How did it make you feel?

Day 3 Money Challenge: *Have a generosity conversation.* If you are married, this needs to be with your spouse. If you are not married, make sure it is with someone who is close to you and knows you well. Discuss God's design for money. Discuss the three-step formula. Finally, ask that person if they are willing to do the challenges with you.

Give Generously

CHAPTER 2

It All Starts Here

Annie found herself back sitting down in front of G.B. after a few days, which made her question her own sanity.

"I did it. Well, *them*. I did all three of them; I did the Money Challenges," Annie said unenthusiastically.

G.B. smiled. "Great! And?"

"I had a conversation with my good friend Martha about the formula you mentioned. Which was fine. Clearly, I don't abide by it now. So that made me feel guilty."

"Do you have people in your life whom you consider generous?"

"Yes."

"How many of them are unhappy and discontent?"

"I don't know. None really. They all seem pretty happy and content."

"It's amazing what happens when the priority for our money is outward-focused. You said that you felt like you were created for more. Remember this—God did not design us to be hoarders, but conduits through which His generosity flows."

Annie typed the statement on her phone.

"Annie, I'm not interested in helping you become financially healthy for the sake of being financially healthy. I want to help you get in a position where you can live out God's design for you and your money. I want to help you live generously."

Annie smirked. "So you aren't going to sell me a credit card?"

G.B. chuckled and shook his head. "Far from it. I want to see you get out of credit card debt, but for the sake of being more open-handed with your resources."

G.B. looked toward the front of the bank and smiled. His next appointment had arrived. He took out his notepad and wrote on it. G.B. ripped the page out.

"Your next Money Challenges," he said, holding the paper out in front of Annie.

Annie took the paper and stood up.

"This is so weird," she said with a partially opened mouth.

G.B. chuckled again. "See you in a couple days."

Annie gave a tight-lipped smile and walked toward the bank's front door.

———

How to Spot a Generous Person

We all have people in our lives we identify as generous. It is not simply because they give away significant amounts of money, though they may. As the story of the widow's gift shows us, those who give away numerically small amounts may actually be the most generous. In God's economy, the amount sacrificed always supersedes the amount given.

For the generous person, their posture of generosity affects all areas of their life, not just their bank account. So, what are some ways we can spot such a person? And what are some generosity identifiers we should consider for our own lives?

First, generous people tend to be satisfied people—except for one thing: the amount they give away.

They always want to give more. They want to be more generous with what they have. They are typically not driven by the desire to acquire more possessions. They may have a nice house, and they may have a nice car. But those things do not *drive* them. They would be just as content without them.

Generous people also say "yes" more than they say "no." Do they have more money than everyone else? No. Do they have more time than everyone else? No. Do they have more possessions than everyone else? No. But they may manage money, time, and possessions in a way that allows them to say, "Yes," more often. And they almost always prioritize people over each one of those areas.

Generous people do not wait for opportunities for generosity to come to them. They ask, "Is there anything I can do for you?" And they *mean* it. They seek out ways in which they can bless others. They know that some of the most needy people will never approach another individual for assistance. Therefore, generosity often involves taking the initiative.

Because they do not think of themselves as owners, they don't talk about "their" possessions. They know that any possession they hold is God's, and it is their responsibility to manage it well for God's purposes. Their possessions are just tools to be used for generosity. They truly believe God did not design us to be hoarders, but conduits through which His generosity flows.

Finally, there is a sense of levity and energy with those who give. Their lack of attachment to possessions develops lightheartedness in them. They are not burdened by the drive to get and keep more stuff. They are not concerned about what others have that they do not, and they live life openhandedly. They experience a freedom and an adventure that most do not.

When individuals align themselves with that design, it becomes obvious. They are easily identified, because their generosity has infected their entire being.

Riches That Last

Matthew 6:20–21 tells us, *"But store up for yourselves treasures in heaven, where neither moth nor rust destroys, and where thieves don't break in and steal. For where your treasure is, there your heart will be also."*

In everything we do and with everything we own, our focus should be to use the resources God has given to make an eternal difference. Sure, most of us will need a place to live and a car to drive.

We will try to help our kids get through college without taking on debt. These are good things. But what if, in the midst of these expenditures, we ask ourselves, "How can I make sure that these expenditures do not derail my ability to live the generous life and to store up for myself treasure in heaven?"

Randy Alcorn says, "Giving is a giant lever positioned on the fulcrum of this world, allowing us to move mountains in the next world. Because we give, eternity will be different—for others and for us."[3]

We were created to live generously. God has given us an incredible opportunity to participate in what He is doing on earth and in heaven. You intuitively knew your resources were meant to be a part of something earth-shattering.

Well, here it is.

The Giving Principles

What is giving even supposed to look like?

Scripture helps us answer that very question. Throughout the Bible, we see a generous God instructing and demonstrating how to live generously. And repeatedly, we see four basic principles for giving.

Principle #1: Giving is to be a priority.

First, giving is to be a priority. The three-step formula starts with giving generously. In the Old Testament, we frequently see God directing the Israelites to give their first and best to Him. They were to give the "first produce" of their harvests (Prov. 3:9).

Whatever crops were produced, the first and best of those crops went to God. This priority is woven throughout the Bible. We were designed to give our first and best to God.

This pattern is completely opposite of what we typically see in our world. We tend to take care of ourselves first and cast off what we have decided we don't need anymore. Giving isn't a driving passion, but it is an afterthought.

So what does the first and best look like for us? For most, this means that some of your *gross salary* (the amount you earn before taxes, insurance, and retirement are taken out) should be given to God's mission. Releasing a part of your gross salary is a way to offer up your first and best. If you are wondering where to give, start with your local church.

Principle #2: Giving is to be done proportionally.

Second, giving is to be done proportionally. You may be familiar with the term *tithe*. Tithe simply means a tenth or 10 percent. In Numbers 18:20–24, God commands the Israelites to give a Levitical Tithe every year. This was to support those who worked in the temple. Other tithes like the Festival Tithe (Deut. 12:17–19) and the Poor Tithe (Deut. 14:28–29) were also commanded by God. The most well-known verse about tithing is Malachi 3:10—*"'Bring the full tenth into the storehouse so that there may be food in my house. Test me in this way,' says the LORD of Armies. 'See if I will not open the floodgates of heaven and pour out a blessing for you without measure.'"*

Within the first few books of the Bible, God lays out a pattern for proportional giving. This means that those who have less are giving less, and those who have more are giving more. God could have said, "Everyone must give $1,000 per year." But He did not. Instead, God asks His people to give in *proportion* to what He has given. There should be a relationship between the amount God gives you to steward and the amount you give to others.

We give because He gave.

There is much debate as to whether or not we should still stick to a strict tithe of 10 percent of our income. Here is my suggestion—if you do not give 10 percent of your gross income, your goal should be to get to that 10 percent mark. If you already give 10 percent of your gross income, it is time to set a new, higher goal. A tithe was never meant to be a limit on your giving.

Principle #3: Giving is to be done sacrificially.

Most, if they give at all, give their leftovers. But we will find our hearts most full when we give our first and best, even if it means we will not be able to purchase something for ourselves later. As we reflect on the story of the widow's mite, we see that God delights in those who give out of sacrifice.

I love David's response when someone tried to give him animals and property for his offering to God:

> *"No, I insist on buying it from you for a price, for I will not offer to the LORD my God burnt offerings that cost me nothing."* (2 Sam. 24:24)

But what should you do when you find yourself financially stressed? Should you really give when times are tough?

When faced with financial difficulties, the question of whether or not to tithe to one's church or to give to others will often arise.

This question is understandable. If you have or are facing financial challenges, you have probably considered not giving. That may seem to be the most logical option for you. But before you decide to abandon your giving, consider the following: *God tells us to give.*

It is not as if the principle that drives Christians to give is commanded by a financial advisor. Giving is not simply "good advice for a happy life." The Bible tells us to give and to do it joyfully. You were designed to live generously, and God does not hide this truth from us. He weaves the concept of giving throughout Scripture.

Remember, giving occurs first, not last.

Giving is not about providing the leftovers. Giving is a prioritized act that often requires sacrifice. Before bills? Yes. Before debt? Yes. Before savings? Yes. Understandably, this prioritized act can be a massive challenge for those in financial distress, but stay with me for a second.

God does not include an exclusion clause.

When the Bible talks about giving, there is no "out." There are no loopholes or exclusion clauses. There are no reasons provided for not giving. We give because He gave so generously to us.

We should not let one bad decision cause us to make another bad decision.

There are cases when financial downfalls are completely out of our hands. But often, we are the cause of our own financial hardship. We buy houses, cars, and clothes we could not afford. We build up balances on high-interest-rate credit cards. Poor financial decisions do not give us reason to make another bad decision—the decision not to give as God desires us to give.

God delights in those who obey when obedience is not convenient.

Let's go back to the story of the widow's gift. We see Jesus point out a poor widow who put two tiny coins into the temple treasury. In the midst of many rich people giving large amounts of money, He says she gave the most because she gave out of sacrifice. She gave when it was inconvenient. If anyone had a reason not to give, it was this widow. But she was obedient, and God saw this obedience and delighted in it.

God will delight in your decision to give even when it is not convenient.

Principle #4: Giving is to be done cheerfully.

Imagine if someone gave you a gift. But instead of doing so in a celebratory manner, they groaned and complained about what it cost them, how they would not be able to do what they really wanted to do now. How would you receive that gift?

I know what I would do. I would ask them to keep it.

God views your giving in the same way. Second Corinthians 9:7 says, *"Each person should do as he has decided in his heart—not reluctantly or out of compulsion, since God loves a cheerful giver."* Your attitude toward giving reflects what you really find most important—God's mission or your wants.

A cheerful attitude toward giving does not negate the fact that real sacrifice is taking place. Cheerful givers can have a lot, have a little, or be in the midst of financial turmoil.

God demonstrated how we are to give when He gave us Jesus. Jesus was His one and only, His first and best. As the owner of everything, He gave us the greatest gift ever given. His sacrifice was the greatest this world has ever seen. And yet, He did it all willingly, purposefully, and cheerfully. Isaiah 53:10 says this:

> *Yet the* LORD *was pleased to crush him severely. When you make him a guilt offering he will see his seed, he will prolong his days, and by his hand the* LORD*'s pleasure will be accomplished.*

Though the sacrifice was great, God gave cheerfully because He looked through the lens of eternity and saw the awesome and worthy outcome. And when we give, so should we.

God didn't just tell us how to give. He showed us. We have a God who gave His first and best and gave proportionally, sacrificially, and cheerfully.

Let's feed the hungry. Let's clothe the naked. Let's make sure we use our resources to make sure that every person on this planet has the opportunity to hear about the love of Jesus. And let's do so by prioritizing proportional, sacrificial, and joyful generosity.

Are you ready for your next Money Challenges?

———

As Annie stepped out of the bank and onto the downtown Chicago sidewalk, she looked at the paper:

Day 4 Money Challenge: *Reflect on God's generosity.* Read Isaiah 53. Consider what His generosity means for your generosity.

Day 5 Money Challenge: *Read Matthew 25:14–30.* Take out a pen and paper and jot down what Jesus is teaching in the Parable of the Talents. Write down what God is impressing on your heart as it relates to your finances.

Day 6 Money Challenge: *Give a gift to a friend or spouse.* Think of something that they would uniquely appreciate. It doesn't necessarily have to cost anything. Be creative and thoughtful.

CHAPTER 3

Let's Get Giving

"The servants. They used the money they were given to increase the master's wealth. It was about him, not them," Annie said as she took her seat in front of G.B.'s desk.

"You're talking about the Parable of the Talents," replied G.B.

"You should know. You gave me the challenge."

G.B. smiled. "Well, you're right. The master gave them the money to use for his purposes."

"It's like God did not design us to be hoarders, but conduits. His generosity flows through us."

"Nicely done, Annie." G.B. was noticeably impressed she remembered what he had said.

"But here's my problem," Annie said with a slightly solemn tone. "I can't be generous. I have no idea how I can come up with

5 percent, 10 percent, 50 percent, or whatever to give. I'm just trying to figure out how to pay my bills."

"I hear that a lot."

"And?"

"And you should try The Takeoff."

"The what?"

"The Takeoff—it's a plan to help you start giving and keep giving. If you aren't giving anything, try to get to 10 percent giving in a year. Start low. Maybe 1 percent and gradually increase it throughout the year. It's like a plane taking off. I think you will find you have more to give than you realize."

"The Takeoff," Annie said, glancing down at the desk.

"That's right. Look, if you wait until you feel like you have enough margin to be generous, you will never be generous. Take a portion of your gross income and give it to your church. We will work on margin, but it's time to start thinking outwardly with your money."

"Yeah, I guess you are right."

G.B. leaned in. "By the way, who is the most generous person you know?"

"Probably Rachel. Why?"

The banker pulled out a piece of paper from the desk's top drawer.

Annie rolled her eyes. "Ah, Money Challenges."

The Takeoff

Do you remember the first time you flew in an airplane?

My first flight was in a small, green prop plane. My dad was the pastor of a small church, and one of the church members owned the plane. He asked if we would like to go up sometime, and, to my excitement, my dad said yes.

A few days later, we found ourselves taxiing out onto a runway in the small plane, my heart rapidly beating with anticipation. We waited until the other planes had cleared the runway, and then it happened. It was our turn to fly.

The propeller buzzed loudly as the plane started moving forward. While the initial trek down the long runway was slow, we started to gain speed. The scenery outside my window began to move more rapidly. In just a few seconds, it was hard to view any particular object for any amount of time.

Suddenly, the small plane angled up, and I could no longer feel the bumps of the runway beneath us. My eyes were wide open, trying to take in the moment. We were flying.

God has designed you to give. He designed giving to take priority and to be done proportionately, sacrificially, and joyfully. But I know that there are many who have never given any of their income to God. For a variety of reasons, the idea of giving gets pushed to the side and often forgotten. Maybe you feel that you can't afford to give. Maybe you have never put much thought into it.

If you have never given, you are missing out. Being generous to your church and others is one of the great joys in life. You get to be a part of Kingdom-advancing adventure. You have to experience it.

Let me introduce to you The Takeoff. The Takeoff is a simple progression that takes you from giving nothing to giving 10 percent of your gross income over twelve months. Like a plane taking off, you start out slow and easy. But over time, as you grow more and more comfortable with giving, momentum will grow. Within a year's time, you will be flying, using part of your income for Kingdom advancement each time you get paid.

As mentioned before, I believe your local church should be the focus of your giving, because the local church is God's primary plan to advance His Kingdom in your community and around the globe. It directly impacts lives on the earth for all eternity. I think that giving 10 percent to your local church is a good initial goal. The Takeoff emphasizes this focus. Let's take a look at the progression:

The Takeoff
- Months 1–3: Give 1% of gross income to your local church.
- Months 4–6: Give 3% of gross income to your local church.
- Months 7–9: Give 5% of gross income to your local church.
- Months 10–11: Give 7% of gross income to your local church.
- Month 12: Give 10% of gross income to your local church.

I know. The thought of not having 10 percent of your paycheck is terrifying. It seems like so much money.

But there is good news. First, you are not alone. Several times I have heard people express that very concern. You can take comfort in knowing that you are not the first person (nor will you be the last) to balk at giving away that portion of your paycheck. Second, I also know many people who, once they started giving, realized they could be generous with more than they had ever imagined. Like The Takeoff, they followed a gradual process. They tested the waters by starting off small and, over time, increased their percentage.

And guess what? They got a taste of what it is like to live generously, and they were hooked. And we know why—because God designed us to be generous. They were experiencing what it means to live a little more openhandedly, and so can you.

Above and Beyond Giving: Those Crazy Macedonians

If the initial goal is to get to 10 percent, what do you do when you actually get there? Or what if you are already there? I know some of you are in this boat. Do you cap your generosity? Can you start to hold your money a little more tightly?

Giving 10 percent of your gross income to your local church is a great thing to do. But it is by no means an end. In fact, the adventure has just begun.

Let's take a look at the crazy generosity of the Macedonians.

In the Bible, we find Paul writing to the church in Corinth:

> *We want you to know, brothers and sisters, about the grace of God that was given to the churches of Macedonia: During a severe trial brought about by affliction, their abundance of joy and their extreme poverty overflowed in a wealth of generosity on their part. I can testify that, according to their ability and even beyond their ability, of*

> *their own accord, they begged us earnestly for the privilege*
> *of sharing in the ministry to the saints.* (2 Cor. 8:1–4)

Did you get that?

The Macedonians suffered from persecution and extreme poverty. They were the last ones you would expect to live generously. But they begged Paul to let their resources be a part of what God was doing in their lifetime. They exuded joyful generosity. This crew was looking to give well beyond 10 percent. The Macedonians wanted to see lives transformed by Christ, and were willing to put everything on the table for God's use.

So what do you do when you reach that level of 10 percent? You consider what's next. You continue prayerfully to explore ways to live generously with your finances. This is your "above-and-beyond" giving. Once you have reached the 10 percent mark, try asking yourself these three questions:

1. Should I give more to my church?

If the local church is God's primary plan to advance His Kingdom in your community and around the globe, should you try to increase your financial participation in your local church?

2. Should I give to another Kingdom-advancing non-profit?

You might be passionate about a specific need in this world. It may be orphan care, feeding the hungry, or providing clean drinking water. There are some great non-profits out there. Should your money go toward one of these causes?

3. Should I set some money aside for unforeseen needs of others?

I call these "ready-to-give opportunities." For this, you would have money reserved so that you are ready and able to help someone in need. Someone you know may not be able to repair his or her car. Someone might not be able to afford groceries. How cool would it be if God used you to help them with their need? What if you had money set aside just so you could assist others in need?

At some level, you'll probably find yourself answering "yes" to all three of those questions. And all are good options.

While I do recommend that the initial 10 percent of your financial generosity go toward your local church, the above-and-beyond portion of your giving may be more divided. You may allocate a portion to your local church and a portion to your favorite Kingdom-advancing non-profit. You may decide to use it all for ready-to-give opportunities. Again, all are great ways to put your money toward something much bigger than yourself. All are opportunities to impact people here on this earth and for all eternity.

The Simple Secrets of Intentional Givers

Have you ever met someone who was accidently generous?

I have yet to run into that person. In fact, I have noticed those who give away the most, tend to be the most intentional about giving. They give *for* a purpose and *on* purpose.

Two challenges many face when trying to move forward in their giving are (1) a lack of consistency and (2) a lack of direction. To combat these challenges, some who have been able to weave giving into the fabric of their lives have two simple secrets—they automate their giving and they have a plan.

Most non-profit organizations, including churches, give you the ability to set up recurring gifts on their website. You simply provide your bank account information and allow them to draw from your account. You can specify the amount you desire to give and the date when it should be drawn. To make it recurring, you will need to specify the frequency of the donation.

If the non-profit does not have the ability to donate on their site, you can often set it up through an online bill pay option with your bank. First, determine the amount you desire to give and when you want to give. Fill out this information on the online bill pay site, and most banks will cut a check on your behalf and send it to the church. Check with your bank and church before setting this up.

Of course, online giving isn't for everyone. If automated giving causes you to no longer think about giving or makes your giving feel disconnected from God's mission, don't do it. Giving is a spiritual act of worship. And I would never advocate for someone to use a method of giving that they feel hinders their spiritual life.

Intentional givers also have a plan. Those who randomly give tend to give less than they realize. It is only until they receive their year-end donation statements do they recognize that, while having great intentions, they donated less than they remembered.

At least once a year, determine your plan for giving. Know how much you plan to give and when. Include above-and-beyond giving. And be able to answer this question: "If I find myself with the ability to give away more, it will go to _____."

Plan to give. And when you are able, make it automatic. These two simple secrets will bring intentionality to your giving.

Let's Get Giving

Aligning with God's design for your money starts here—giving generously. It is the sun around which everything else revolves. We manage our money in a way that allows us to be generous to our church and to others. It should be on the forefront of our minds as we make decisions about getting rid of debt, saving for the future, and day-to-day living expenditures.

Generosity is the "why" behind becoming financially healthy. Now let's take a look at your upcoming Money Challenges.

———

As Annie read her next Money Challenges, she pulled up Rachel's phone number.

Day 7 Money Challenge: *Spend some time with the most generous person you know.* Share a meal or have a cup of coffee. Let them know in advance that you want to learn how to be more generous. Treat it like an interview. Ask questions and just listen. Soak in their words.

Day 8 Money Challenge: *It's time to take off.* Set yourself up to have at least 1 percent from your gross monthly pay given away. I recommend that you start with your local church. Remember, consider making it automatic.

Save Wisely

CHAPTER 4

Ants in Your Pants

Annie walked into the bank disheveled and clearly agitated.

"I'm sorry I'm so late. My car broke down. I knew it would happen sooner or later." The frustration in her voice was evident. "Of course, I have no money to fix it. So, here's to more debt."

She raised her hand as if sarcastically giving a toast.

"I'm sorry, Annie," replied G.B.

"Well, at least I gave to my church. Boy, that sure seems like a smart move now." Annie sarcastically sighed.

"Again, I'm sorry, Annie. It is right to give to your church. It is your financial priority. But life still happens. I assume you didn't have any savings."

"Of course not."

"Where did you take your car?"

"Terry's Auto Shop. It's a local place."

G.B. nodded his head.

"Please know that I am not trying to be insensitive to your situation, but this does bring up an important point. We are to give generously, but we are also to save wisely. Remember—*give generously, save wisely, and live appropriately.*"

"You know, I'm really not in the mood to hear this."

"I understand. Here, take this with you. I will see you in a few days."

G.B. handed Annie the next Money Challenges.

"Annie, when you started giving, you took a big step in getting closer to God's design for your money. Don't stop now."

Why We Don't Save

We are first to give generously and then to save wisely.

But we struggle with saving money. In the U.S., most would not be able to pay for a financial emergency that costs more than $400.[4] There is just not enough money in the majority of people's bank accounts to cover it.

It's a scary thought.

So why is it that we don't save? Let's look at a few common reasons why people don't set aside money for the future.

First is the desire for instant gratification. Instant gratification is getting what you want, when you want it. Never before has this been more of a possibility than today. For better or worse, credit cards, the Internet, and expedited shipping have opened up a whole new world where you can get almost anything delivered to your doorstep the next day or sooner.

Immediacy is now an expectation, and has given way to a sense of entitlement.

Of course, instant gratification is not just about purchasing stuff. We want to gain experiences. And we don't want to wait until we are older. We want to travel. We want to live in a really expensive city. We want to taste the "good life."

As we try to satisfy these wants now, we push savings off until later.

The second reason we don't save is the inability to grasp future reality. There is a lack of understanding when it comes to short-term and long-term saving needs. Most people significantly underestimate the amount of money they need to save, and how long it will take them to set aside that much money.

Sometimes, we simply ignore the reality of a future need altogether. We would rather not think about a financial emergency or retirement because it's not fun to think about it. To be honest, the idea can be daunting and even discouraging. So we punt on the idea of saving, creating an even larger problem.

The third reason we don't save is a lack of financial margin. You have too many expenditures and too little money. There is no margin, so you can't save.

Sometimes this reality is the result of spending habits, and sometimes it is the result of financial circumstances beyond your control. As we walk through this book, I hope you will find ways to create and increase the margin in your finances.

Fortunately, in the midst of our struggle to save, the Bible talks to us about setting aside money for the future. God, the owner of it all, gives us guidance in this difficult area of our finances.

And His teaching involves a tiny, little insect.

Ants, the Bible, and Savings

Did you know some people have claimed that there are more than 12,000 ant species around the world? Others have said there are so many ants on our planet that the combined weight of all ants is close to the combined weight of all humans. Regardless, one of the most amazing abilities ants have is the ability to lift items significantly heavier than themselves. Ants can lift anywhere between ten to fifty times their own body weight.

Pretty incredible stuff.

Ants go out and return to their homes with a seemingly resilient purpose—acquire and bring back food. Throughout history, ants have been used to illustrate persistency and consistency.

King Solomon, known for his wisdom, used ants as an analogy for those who save for the future. Let's take a look at some of the verses found in the book of Proverbs that encourage saving:

> *Go to the ant, you slacker! Observe its ways and become wise. Without leader, administrator, or ruler, it prepares its provisions in summer; it gathers its food during harvest.* (Prov. 6:6–8)

Four things on earth are small, yet they are extremely wise: ants are not a strong people, yet they store up their food in the summer. (Prov. 30:24–25)

So what does God teach us about saving? Here are five lessons we learn:

1. **Saving is wise.** Setting aside money for future purposes is a good decision. It demonstrates solid judgment. Like a hurricane coming toward the coast, you know that large expenditures are on their way. And preparation is the best way to avoid significant damage.

2. **There are seasons of abundance and seasons of scarcity.** Like the ant in summer, most of us will go through times when work and money just seem to be obtained more easily than other times. Likewise, most of us will go through times when both jobs and money seem scarce.

3. **Abundance gives you an opportunity to prepare for scarcity.** Leverage the good seasons. An increase in your paycheck should not immediately create an increase in your spending. Take advantage of the opportunity to set money aside.

4. **Saving requires a goal.** There should be purpose to your savings. There should be direction. We will walk through some of these goals in the upcoming chapters.

5. **Saving requires persistence.** Setting aside a little bit of money over a long period of time makes a big difference. There is great power in habitual savings. This possibility is especially true if you are young.

The Bible encourages us to save for future expenditures, and it does so in a very clear way. But the Bible does not, however, say that saving money is easy.

Nobody taunts the ant as it carries a piece of food that is fifty times its own body weight. Why? Because that ant is doing something incredibly difficult! And, yet, that ant is also doing something that is incredibly important.

Saving money is not always easy, but it is important. And its importance is not just found in the ability to be prepared for future expenditures, although that is important. The need for preparation does so much more than just having enough for future expenditures.

What if I told you that saving money can make us freer to give?

What if I told you that saving money can help you make an eternal difference in the lives of those in your community and around the world?

Save to Give

A book titled *The Millionaire Next Door* by Thomas Stanley and William Danko shows us that most real millionaires go unnoticed. They don't live extravagantly. They don't purchase new cars. They don't have mansions. They are frugal people who save well. And this is exactly how they became millionaires.

I don't know if Don was a millionaire or not, but he fits the mold of most real millionaires. I met Don a few years ago. And, man, I'm glad I did. Don was living proof of the power of persistent saving. He is now in his sixties and retired, and no one would ever consider his past career as a lucrative route. He was an electrician.

And from what I could tell, a pretty good one. But even good electricians don't find themselves earning million-dollar salaries.

Yet, Don no longer had to work to make a living. Instead, he spent his days volunteering at his local church, taking care of the church's facilities. If something broke, he was there to fix it. He worked on big projects and small ones. He was a huge blessing to the church.

Don was giving and saving with open hands.

He was living generously.

So how did Don get here? If you were to ask him his secret, what would he tell you?

He would tell you that it wasn't that complicated.

Don saved. He lived frugally, limited his debt, and saved for retirement. He was the human version of the ant we see in the Bible. Now he experiences a life and a level of Kingdom-advancing generosity that most dream about. It wasn't about the amount of money he made, but the way he managed what he had been given.

When we set aside money for the future, we are freeing ourselves up for greater, future generosity. This happens because the absence of savings often leads to credit card debt and loans.

Here's how it works: You don't have any money saved for emergencies, and then your car engine dies on the interstate. So you turn to credit cards.

You don't have any money set aside for your child's college tuition. So you and your child turn to student loans.

You never invested much in your retirement account. So you have to keep working to pay the bills.

And as you pay the interest on the credit card balances and student loans, or as you work in your life's later years, you will realize that not saving is actually an expensive endeavor.

So why do we save?

Certainly, we save to prepare ourselves for future events. But there is more. We save to give. We save so that we can live generously. We prepare for the future so that we don't use an unnecessary amount of money and time on the inevitable. Setting aside our money ends up freeing future money and time that can be used to live generously.

Become like Don

How do you become like Don? How do you lessen the impact that a car repair, medical expense, tuition costs, or job loss can have on your finances? How do you save to give?

When it comes to saving, we must consider how to save for now and for later.

In the next two chapters, we will discuss how to prepare for both categories.

God designed you to be a conduit through which His generosity flows. Don followed the ant's example and experiences this now.

So can you.

God's formula for managing money starts with giving generously. But then we are to save wisely. And we save wisely because it allows us to spend less and give more. We can be more openhanded with our money and our time.

Before we dive into the next chapter, you have some things to do.

Are you ready for your next Money Challenges?

———

Though she was frustrated, Annie read her next challenges:

Day 9 Money Challenge: *Write 2 Corinthians 9:7 on a note card and put it on your bathroom mirror.* Let it remind you how giving should occur for each of us. Pray that God can make you a cheerful giver. We save wisely so we can give joyfully.

Day 10 Money Challenge: *Put others first, literally.* Next time you are in line, let the person behind you go first. And if you have the opportunity, hold the door for someone, making sure that they enter through the doorway ahead of you.

CHAPTER 5

Expect the Unexpected

"Well, you look better than you did a few days ago," G.B. said as Annie took her seat.

"I am. You know, the weirdest thing happened after I left the bank the other day. I received a phone call from the car repair mechanic. He was supposed to let me know how much the repair would cost. I did mention to him that money was tight and how I was walking through this Money Challenge thing, but that was it. And after he told me what needed to be done, he said that the repair cost was already taken care of."

"Wow! That's great news, Annie."

"I know, right? I am still in shock. It's so weird. I wonder who paid the bill?"

G.B. gave a smile. "Can you imagine if, instead of living on the financial edge all the time, you were in the position to help someone like you?"

Annie's smile relaxed. Her eyes gazed down, and an unexpected image of Randall, the kind homeless man, ran through her mind.

"It would be incredible," she said contemplatively.

"Do you remember the three-step formula found in the Bible?"

"Give generously, save wisely, and live appropriately."

"You got it. Look, I know this will sound crazy, but in order to give generously, you have to save wisely. Constantly living on the edge of financial ruin causes you to hold everything tightly. To live with open hands, you must step away from the edge. You have to save."

"I guess it makes sense."

"Trust me. It helps your ability to be generous. You need an emergency savings account. Start with a $1,500 goal. After that, you'll work to save three to six months of living expenses."

"I don't know if I can do that."

"You can. Just focus on the $1,500 for now."

G.B. placed on the desk in front of Annie a folded piece of paper—her Money Challenges. Before Annie could pick it up, G.B. patted the piece of paper, and with a look of assurance in his eyes said, "You really can do this, Annie."

Annie smirked and slowly nodded her head. What a whirlwind these past few days had been for her. And yet, she could sense that something was changing. She just couldn't pin down what it was.

This Is an Emergency

Over the next twelve months, you will probably run into an unexpected expense. You don't know what it will be or how much it will cost you, but it is lurking, ready to surprise you.

That's not a fun thing to accept.

But just consider the past year. Did you anticipate every expense? Or were there a few surprises? If you were like most of us, you had a few unexpected and unwelcome expenditures. The water heater went out. The car broke down. You got really sick. Your work hours were reduced. You lost your job.

What happened when those expenses hit? Were you able to cover them with cash, or did you find yourself struggling to pay the bills and diving into credit card debt?

Your answer to that question is probably determined by whether or not you had an *emergency fund*. An emergency fund is simply a lump of money set aside to help you cover unanticipated expenses. This would fall into the short-term saving category, though we will talk later in the book about long-term strategies.

Emergency funds are considered one of the basic and critical building blocks of financial health. Emergency funds help you avoid accumulating credit card balances with high interest rates or taking out loans. I am sure you can find better ways to use your money than on interest payments. Remember, we save to give.

This means that you should have an emergency fund.

There are two different levels of emergencies to consider when creating an emergency fund—minor and job loss emergencies.

Minor emergency ($1,500). A minor emergency is an unexpected expense that costs $1,500 or less. This may include car repairs, kitchen appliance repairs, or medical bills. While these types of emergencies are less expensive, they tend to be the most frequent level of emergency. Fortunately, because they are often less expensive, financial recovery is typically quicker than the other types of emergencies.

Job loss (3 to 6 months' worth of living expenses). Losing a job has the potential to send your world into a whirlwind. It is emotionally and financially draining. You need to find work. You may need to sell your house and move. You may need to find a new school for your kids. Just thinking about it is exhausting. And if you don't find a job right away, any money you've saved will quickly get spent.

Understanding the different emergency levels will help you set future saving goals. But I am sure you have some questions right now about emergency savings.

Emergency Fund Questions

There are many good questions surrounding emergency funds. Let's explore at least three common emergency fund questions.

How Much?

A frequent question about emergency funds is, "How do I decide how much? Is it three, four, five, or six months?" This is a great question.

If you are only financially responsible for yourself, then lean more toward a three-month emergency savings fund. A person who is just responsible for himself or herself can typically be more financially agile than others. However, as you become financially responsible for others, maybe a spouse and then children, you will need to move more toward the six-month end of the scale. So let the weight of your financial responsibility determine where you need to land within the three-to-six-month savings range.

Where?

Where do you put the emergency funds? Do you put them in a checking account, savings account, CD, or investment account? This is another good question.

You want your emergency savings fund to be easily accessible. When your car breaks down, you need your money immediately. The most easily accessed accounts are going to be checking or savings accounts. So my preference is to have the majority of emergency funds in a savings account, especially if you have yet to save three to six months' worth of living expenses.

Do I Save before I Pay Off My Debt?

Or, do you need to pay off your debt before you start your emergency savings?

Certainly, you need to pay off your debt quickly, especially debt such as credit card balances that carry a high interest rate. However, this does not remove your need for an emergency fund. Here is what I suggest:

1. Make sure you are giving. This is your financial priority. If you don't currently give, start somewhere. The Takeoff is a good way to do this.

2. Save enough money for a minor emergency. This is $1,500. Do this before you start putting additional money toward your debts. Of course, continue to make your minimum payment during this time.

3. If your employer offers a retirement contribution match, take it. Contribute whatever is necessary to receive the maximum match. We will address this in more detail in the next chapter.

4. Get rid of your debts. Later in the book, we will discuss the Snowball Method, which is the best way to do this. Debt is a generosity killer.

5. Prepare for a "job loss emergency level." This can be anywhere from three to six months' worth of living expenses, depending on how many people are dependent on your paycheck.

If you happen to receive a bonus at work or some other type of financial windfall, take full advantage of it. Don't go out and buy stuff you don't need. Use it to reach whatever next step you can in building an emergency fund. Either pay off your debt or put it in your savings account.

If possible, postpone major purchases like cars and furniture until you reach the job-loss-emergency level. You will want to pay for these with cash so any purchase could significantly derail your emergency fund saving.

After you give, save. This starts with your emergency fund. Remember, you will have some type of financial emergency, you just don't know what it is yet. I hope it is in the far future, but it might be just around the corner. Protect yourself and those who rely on you.

Get your emergency fund going.

———

As she pushed the bank's door to exit the building, Annie read her next Money Challenges.

Day 11 Money Challenge: *Determine how much you need for your emergency (3–6 months) savings account.* If you have kids, I recommend landing on an amount that is closer to the six-month mark.

Day 12 Money Challenge: *Set up your emergency savings account.* Find an account that requires a very small minimum balance to avoid any fees. Place the minimum amount in it to get started. Then, set up a monthly transfer from your checking to your savings.

CHAPTER 6

Your $600,000 Plan

"Don't you think it would have been more efficient for me to just set up my emergency savings account with you before I left last time?" Annie jokingly asked with squinted eyes as she pressed her pointer finger against her lips.

G.B. laughed. "Probably. Do you want to open one now?"

"Well, it would be nice of you." Annie gave a tight-lipped smile.

G.B. started quickly typing on his computer. It was clear that this was not the first account he had opened. As he typed, he talked. "So you also need to start thinking about retirement."

"I don't think I am ready quite yet. I still have a few more years in me." Annie smiled. She was in a good mood today.

"Not now. Later. But you need to start saving as soon as possible. Time can be your best friend; once your emergency fund is set up, focus on retirement."

Out of the corner of her eye, Annie saw a person she knew. It was the pastor of her church, Pastor John. He was older, probably in his late sixties. He had this deep, loud voice that was perfect for preaching, or a movie trailer. Annie loved Pastor John. She waved, which caught his attention. Pastor John smiled and walked over to her and G.B.

"Hey, Annie and G.B.!"

For some reason, Annie was surprised that he knew G.B. But then she realized that pastors needed banks too.

"Hello, Pastor. It's good to see you," Annie replied.

"What are you two discussing?" Pastor John questioned.

"Savings and retirement," G.B. interjected while still typing on his computer.

"Ah. Listen to him, Annie. He knows his stuff. I wish I knew at your age what I know now. Set aside money for retirement now. Don't be like me."

Pastor John paused.

"Annie, some of the most difficult challenges I have faced are financial. Financial decisions expose our deepest desires and our deepest idols. Though it might seem like it at times, saving for the future is not a spirit-less endeavor, but profoundly spiritual.

"When you read in the Bible about harvests and planting and sowing seeds—you ought to see salary and mutual funds and investment accounts. You see, the economy of the Bible is agrarian (meaning farming-centered), but the economy of our world is more specialized. God recorded the principles G.B. is teaching you in the Scriptures!

"Part of the reason I didn't plan for the future was because I was careless. It wasn't that I was money-obsessed, but money-less. So I submitted myself to denial. But that decision not only affected me; it affected my wife, my kids, even my grandkids. And I don't have to tell you, that decision was neither kind nor gentle nor patient nor . . . well, you get the picture."

Annie replied, "Thank you, Pastor."

The transparency caught Annie off guard. She wanted to say something, but Pastor John continued.

"I will probably never retire. I thought not worrying about money was a good thing. Now I realize there is a big difference between not *worrying* and not *caring*. I should have cared more."

Pastor John went over and patted G.B. on the back. "You are a good man."

G.B. smiled. "All right, Annie. You have a new savings account."

He handed her some papers for the new account. The top piece was folded.

"That top one is for the next two days," G.B. said. "You need to start thinking about your future."

Annie opened up the paper to read the Money Challenges. But then Pastor John's loud, deep voice made her jump. "Do it, Annie!" Pastor John said, chuckling with a huge smile.

Annie couldn't help but laugh with him.

She was thankful for her pastor.

Ready to Cringe?

Let's play the "what if" game.

Some of you may be familiar with the term "compounding." It is a pretty simple concept. The percentage you earn each year is placed on your principal (the amount you contributed). So the next year, your gain is not just based on the principal, but the total amount of principal plus whatever gains you had. Over time, you can see significant growth occur.

Here's a quick example—If you had $100 and earned 10 percent in year one, you end year one with $110. Then, let's say you also earn 10 percent in year two. Since you started year two with $110, the 10 percent now gets you $11 ($110 x 10 percent). You end year two with $121. Over time a 10 percent increase will give you a larger and larger gain.

That's compounding in a nutshell.

Now let's consider some real-life numbers.

Let's suppose you get your first job at age sixteen. Instead of wasting all your money trying to customize the beat-up car your parents let you drive, you open a retirement account and place $2,000 in a mutual fund that mimics the annual return of the S&P 500 (a benchmark of the U.S. stock market performance) from 1966 to 2015. You add $2,000 at ages seventeen and eighteen. Before you leave for college, what have you accomplished?

Check out the chart on the next page.

Age	Contribution	S&P Return	Growth
16	$2,000.00	−9.97%	$1,800.60
17	$2,000.00	23.80%	$4,705.14
18	$2,000.00	10.81%	$7,429.97
19	$0.00	−8.24%	$6,817.74
20	$0.00	3.56%	$7,060.45
21	$0.00	14.22%	$8,064.45
22	$0.00	18.76%	$9,577.34
23	$0.00	−14.31%	$8,206.82
24	$0.00	−25.90%	$6,081.25
25	$0.00	37%	$8,331.32
26	$0.00	23.83%	$10,316.67
27	$0.00	−6.98%	$9,596.57
28	$0.00	6.51%	$10,221.30
29	$0.00	18.52%	$12,114.29
30	$0.00	31.74%	$15,959.36
31	$0.00	−4.70	$15,209.27
32	$0.00	20.42%	$18,315.01
33	$0.00	22.34%	$22,406.58
34	$0.00	6.15%	$23,784.59
35	$0.00	31.24%	$31,214.89
36	$0.00	18.49%	$36,986.52
37	$0.00	5.81%	$39,135.44
38	$0.00	16.54%	$45,608.44
39	$0.00	31.48%	$59,965.98
40	$0.00	−3.06%	$58,131.02
41	$0.00	30.23%	$75,704.03
42	$0.00	7.49%	$81,374.26
43	$0.00	9.97%	$89,487.27
44	$0.00	1.33%	$90,677.45
45	$0.00	37.20%	$124,409.47
46	$0.00	22.68%	$152,625.53
47	$0.00	33.10%	$203,144.59
48	$0.00	28.34%	$260,715.76
49	$0.00	20.89%	$315,179.29
50	$0.00	−9.03%	$286,718.60
51	$0.00	−11.85%	$252,742.44
52	$0.00	−21.97%	$197,214.93
53	$0.00	28.36%	$253,145.08
54	$0.00	10.74%	$280,332.86
55	$0.00	4.83%	$293,872.94
56	$0.00	15.61%	$339,746.51
57	$0.00	5.48%	$358,364.61
58	$0.00	−36.55%	$227,382.35
59	$0.00	25.94%	$286,365.33
60	$0.00	14.82%	$328,804.67
61	$0.00	2.10%	$335,709.57
62	$0.00	15.89%	$389,053.82
63	$0.00	32.15%	$514,134.62
64	$0.00	13.52%	$583,645.62
65	$0.00	1.36%	**$591,583.20**

Well done. You just gave yourself almost $600,000 for retirement by contributing $6,000 prior to college. Not bad for a summer job. And what if you developed a habit of putting $2,000 each year into the account? You could be a millionaire by age sixty-five.

These types of charts are illustrations to demonstrate the power of starting early, so the numbers aren't set in stone. Certainly, mutual funds fluctuate in price. Like the S&P 500, some years have positive growth while others have negative growth. These fluctuations would influence the overall value of the fund at age sixty-five. But the point remains—start early, start early, and start early.

Now, you may not be sixteen anymore when you are reading this, but that doesn't mean you shouldn't go ahead and start now. Time is one of your greatest resources when it comes to investing.

Retirement

In the blink of an eye, you will be packing up your office, with thank-you notes littering your desk, and a congratulations banner and half-eaten cake left in the break room. And for better or worse, you will reap the financial fruit of the decisions you are making today.

Retirement may seem far in the future, but it is closer than you think. Life moves fast. When it comes to saving for later, retirement is your most pressing issue. And as you just saw, the earlier you start saving for retirement, the better.

Retirement plans can get confusing, so hang with me. I will try to keep it simple. Let's start by looking at two basic categories of retirement plans: employer-sponsored and personal plans.

Employer-Sponsored Plans

Employer-sponsored plans are those plans that are available to you through your work. In other words, if you did not work at that particular company or organization, you would not be able to contribute to the plan.

The three most common employer-sponsored plans are 401(k)s, 403(b)s, and 457(b)s. The one you have will depend on the type of workplace—for profit, non-profit, or public sector. The ways they work are similar. You place pre-tax dollars into these plans. Most of the time this is taken directly from your paycheck. Once in the plan, you choose an investment, probably a mutual fund, which the plan offers.

For both the 401(k) and 403(b), there is a 10 percent penalty if you withdraw funds from the plan before age 59½. You will also have to pay ordinary income tax on the amount you withdraw. For a 457(b), there is no penalty, but you do have to pay ordinary income tax. But if you happen to reach 70½ years old before you withdraw anything from these plans, the government will require you to do so at that time.

Personal Plans

Personal plans are not attached to any employer, and you can choose any type of investment you like. You are not limited to a select group of investments like the employer-sponsored plans. There are two primary types of individual retirement accounts (IRAs)—Traditional and Roth.

Contributions to a Traditional IRA can be tax deductible. In the plan, your investments grow tax-deferred, meaning you get taxed when you withdraw the funds. Unlike the Roth IRA, there are no income limitations for you to contribute. However, there is a yearly maximum contribution. For 2016, this maximum was $5,500 and $6,500 for those over fifty years old. If you withdraw money before you turn 59½, there is a 10 percent penalty in addition to your regular income taxes.

Money contributed to a Roth IRA is after-tax. Because of this, the major benefit of a Roth IRA is that when you get to 59½, you can remove the funds tax-free. The maximum contributions are the same as the Traditional IRA, but there are income limitations. Like the Traditional plan, if you withdraw money before 59½, you get hit with a 10 percent penalty.

So which one do I choose? Good question. Let me answer by first talking about employer matches. Some employers will match some or all of your employer-sponsored plan contributions up to a certain percent of your salary. For example, ABC Company may match $0.50 for every dollar you contribute up to 5 percent of your salary. So if your salary is $50,000, and you contribute 5 percent of your salary ($2,500) in a year, ABC Company will throw in an additional $1,250 into your plan. It is an incredible deal. You just received a guaranteed 50 percent return on the money you contributed!

If your company matches, be sure to get that money. Do not leave it on the table. Make sure you contribute whatever amount it takes to get that whole match. It is the best investment you will make.

If your company does not match, make sure to pay off your debt (excluding your mortgage) and save three to six months of living expenses before contributing to a retirement account. If you have done this and are under the Roth IRA income limitations, open up a Roth IRA and start contributing.

How much should I save? This is another great question. Try to work your way to 15 percent of your salary.

I know. It's a big chunk. But consider this—for your retirement funds to produce $50,000 per year without affecting your core funds, you will need $1 million earning 5 percent a year in retirement. If you want $100,000, you will need $2 million.

The time to get started is now. Get your employer's match and then focus on your Roth IRA.

Saving for College

College tuition. These two words strike fear in the hearts of parents.

In 1996, the Internal Revenue Service (IRS) allowed for states to operate college savings plans. My favorite is the 529 Plan. These investment plans were given the name 529 because they came from Section 529 in the U.S. tax code. Creative, right?

The way it works is simple. You set up a plan for a single beneficiary. For most, this will be your child. The plans allow for after-tax contributions, and these contributions are placed into an investment fund (so, yes, there is risk involved). Some states let you select from a few funds; others don't. All growth within the plan and withdrawals are tax-free. When Susie is ready for college, you are able to withdraw from the account, tax-free, as long as the money is used for qualified expenditures (tuition, fees, books, supplies, and equipment required by the school).

So why should you consider setting up a 529 Plan? Here are a few reasons.

- **Tax-free withdrawal is a really big deal.** The last thing you need is for the government to take part of your college investment earnings. But that is exactly what will happen if you use a regular investment account or place money in a CD. You will be taxed on your wise decision to set aside money for college. 529 Plans protect you from this.

- **You are not stuck with your state's plan.** In fact, you can choose any state plan you want. Do you live in Tennessee but like Alaska's plan? You can get Alaska's plan. Or Maryland's. Or Utah's. And you are not stuck with one account either. You can have multiple 529 Plans from various states for a single beneficiary. What would drive you to another state's plan? The key factor in determining which plan to choose—performance.

- **You can change beneficiaries.** What if Susie doesn't go to college? What if she gets a full scholarship? Or what if you don't use all of the funds in Susie's 529 Plan? You can change beneficiaries. They must be a member of the beneficiary's family. This includes siblings, parents, stepparents, nephews, nieces, aunts, uncles, in-laws, and first cousins.

- **Many allow anyone to contribute.** If others want to contribute to the beneficiary's college savings, they can. Of course, they will lose control of funds. If the plan does not allow others to contribute, they can always set up their own 529 Plan for the same beneficiary.

- **There are some great sites out there to guide you along.** My favorite site is savingforcollege.com. It is rich with information and can help find a 529 Plan that works for you.

Saving for college is a daunting task. And if you are a parent with multiple kids, it can be a terrifying thought. Many try not to think about it. However, the worst thing you can do is ignore the financial reality that looms. Avoiding your financial reality is a sure way to avoid financial success. Whether you choose a 529 Plan or not, start setting aside money for college expenses. Your future self will be glad you did.

Retirement or College Savings?

I love being a dad. As a parent, I can understand the desire to set money aside for your kids before yourself. Yet, while the desire is noble, it is not best for you or your kids. You know how flight attendants tell you to put your oxygen mask on before putting them on your kids? It's kind of like that. Let's think this through together.

First, remember the importance of starting early. The more you invest early, the better off you will be. Discontinuing your retirement savings in lieu of your kids' college savings will cause you to miss out on some key retirement saving years. You may not notice the impact now, but you will at age sixty-five.

Second, your financial future can affect their financial future. More and more, kids are tasked with physically and financially caring for their elderly parents. You can help their future financial situation by doing everything you can to take care of yours.

Third, it is easier to pay for college than retirement. College is expensive, but not as expensive as retirement. If you want to retire, you must have a substantial amount of money set aside.

Fourth, paying for your kids' college is nice but not mandatory. You are not a bad parent if you cannot pay for your kids' college. Certainly, it would be a blessing. But there are plenty of college students with great parents who cannot afford to cover the high costs of college.

And finally, being financially responsible teaches your kids to be financially responsible. Prioritizing your retirement over your kids' college savings is not selfish. It really is the best financial decision for you and your family. Hopefully, when your kids see you making good money decisions, they will be encouraged to do the same.

I know placing your retirement over your kids' college savings goes against your natural desire. Trust me, I get it. But it is a decision that will benefit your kids long after they put on their graduation regalia and receive their hard-earned diplomas.

Let's Prepare for the Future

We set aside money now so we can be even more generous later. Long-term savings will result in long-term generosity. Do not get caught off guard when your kids' college or your retirement arrives. Prepare for the future.

Are you up for the challenge?

With a smile on her face, Annie looked back down to read her next Money Challenges.

Day 13 Money Challenge: *Find out how much you need for retirement.* There are plenty of great retirement calculators available online, like the one on BankRate.com. Enter the necessary information to determine where you currently stand with your retirement savings. Next, determine how much you will need to start setting aside to retire comfortably at age sixty-five.

Day 14 Money Challenge: *Set up your retirement account.* If your company offers one, talk to your Human Resources office and get enrolled. If they don't offer one, set up a low-cost Roth IRA. Start working toward your 15 percent goal.

Live Appropriately

CHAPTER 7

We Are Rich

"Whoa. What is that?"

Annie tried to figure out what G.B. was referring to. She had just arrived.

"What is what?" she responded.

"That phone you just set down on the desk. When did you get it?"

"Oh. I bought it on the way here. My old phone had a cracked screen on it. How it got there is a long story. But I needed a new phone, so I bought one."

"But that isn't just any phone. It just came out, right? That is probably the most expensive one on the market."

"I suppose so."

"Well, why did you get that particular phone?"

"I don't know. One of my coworkers had one. And I liked it. So I thought I would get one too." She suddenly realized where G.B. was going with his questioning. "I guess I could have made a better financial decision. Geez. Thanks for the buzzkill."

"Look, I'm not trying to depress you. I just really want to see you aligning with God's design for you and your money."

"I know, I know. God designed us not to be hoarders, but conduits through which His generosity flows."

G.B. raised his eyebrows. "Exactly. This is why we *give generously, save wisely,* and *live appropriately.*"

"I suppose that buying a super expensive phone when you are struggling to pay your bills doesn't fit under 'living appropriately.'"

"Probably not. Living appropriately is managing your resources in a way that is both financially healthy and Kingdom-advancing. Your lifestyle can either help or hurt your ability to live generously."

"Hmm. Sounds like I have some work to do in this area."

"Don't worry. We will talk more about it next time. The important thing to remember is that your lifestyle decisions have a huge impact on your financial well-being and generosity. Let me give you your next challenges."

He handed over the paper with its familiar fold.

Annie took it. "Thanks. I guess I have a phone to return and a cheaper one to buy."

G.B. grinned at Annie. "Now that sounds like a good decision to me."

Living Appropriately

We are to *give generously* and *save wisely*. But what does it look like to *live appropriately*? This is a big question, because the lifestyle we choose to live and the purchases we choose to make will have a dramatic effect on whether or not we are able to give and save.

Living appropriately is managing your resources in a way that is both financially healthy and Kingdom-advancing. It is having the right perspective on the resources you have and the resources you will purchase. In this chapter, we are going to look at what it means to live appropriately.

Living appropriately means having a realistic view of possessions.

Marsha Richins, a University of Missouri professor, did some research on people who place great, transformative hope on their purchases.[5] They hope the possessions can change how others perceive them, better their relationships, indicate success, and make life more enjoyable. Most would define these people as materialists.

Through her research, Richins uncovered that those who put great weight on their purchases reported high levels of joy, excitement, contentment, and optimism prior to buying the item. They couldn't wait to get their new item.

But then something happened.

As purchases were made, the joy, excitement, contentment, and optimism of those who put great, personal hope on the purchases began to drop. And within just a short period of time after the purchase, all of these feelings had fallen significantly.

What transpired?

Simple. The transformative hope they had placed on the item did not happen. The hope of everything they thought their purchase could do for them did not become reality.

Stuff became stuff.

So, when it comes to living appropriately, we should start here.

One of the great challenges to living appropriately is our view on the items we purchase. Sometimes, we create unrealistic expectations on how a new car or a larger home will make us feel about ourselves. We imagine how driving that car or walking around that larger home will make us feel more successful and happier.

But the happiness is short-lived. Inevitably, the purchases let us down.

We all dive headfirst into whatever we identify as the hope for our lives. If we view possessions as our hope to make life more enjoyable, we can easily justify doing whatever it takes to get that item, including disregarding sound, financial decision-making.

Those who live appropriately find their hope in something other than what they buy. They have a realistic view of possessions. The items they purchase are not their hope for a more enjoyable life.

Stuff is just stuff.

Living appropriately means knowing what you can afford.

You have probably heard it said, "Live within your means." Whether we have much or little, we all have a limit. None of us can afford everything. Living within your means means spending less than you make.

You may struggle with debt. You might have purchased more than you could afford. You lived beyond your means. And you are paying for it, usually with a high interest rate.

Those who live appropriately know how much they can spend. They know their financial capacity. If a purchase pushes them beyond their limit, they don't buy it.

Of course, this type of decision-making requires some planning. We will get to that in the next chapter.

Living appropriately means understanding the impact of purchases on giving and saving.

Knowing what you can and cannot afford increases your ability to give and save. Often, we don't really think about giving and saving until after we have made our purchases. We wait until the end of the month and see what is left over.

Those who live appropriately see this as backwards. They consider what they give and what they save as money that is already accounted for. They adjust their expenditures to accommodate their giving and saving, not vice versa. This way, they are always giving generously and saving wisely.

And they are also living more fulfilled.

Living appropriately means finding greater fulfillment in advancing God's Kingdom rather than building your own kingdom.

God has designed us to experience fulfillment when we seek out His purposes and are a part of His mission. When we move away from this, we find ourselves dissatisfied with ourselves, others, and life in general. We find ourselves empty, sensing that we are missing out on something.

It's exactly because we are missing out on something.

Those who choose to live appropriately for the sake of God's mission find great fulfillment in their decision. They don't worry about what type of earthly kingdom they are building for themselves because they know that earthly kingdoms are temporary and empty. They know that advancing God's Kingdom is where the real adventure and satisfaction is found.

Living appropriately means asking a better question.

One of the most challenging thoughts on generosity that I have come across is found in a book titled *God and Money*.[6] The authors were both Harvard MBAs on the track to, what most would see as career and financial success.

As part of a project, they studied the Bible's teachings on money. While they scoured through Scripture, they began to consider that maybe we've been asking poor questions.

Most of us ask, "How much should I give?" This is a good question with good motives. But it might not be the best question. A better question may be, "How much should I keep?"

This question flies in the face of typical messaging in which we are told to accumulate as much stuff as possible. There is great freedom in determining your lifestyle limit. It frees you from trying to keep up with the world around you. It frees you to be more generous. It frees you to invest in eternal causes.

I am not advocating for a specific limit. That is between you and God.

I am suggesting that you consider a limit. Those who live appropriately have a limit on their lifestyle. It is the limit that frees them. Those who live appropriately ask a better question.

We Are All Wealthy

Can someone be both wealthy and generous?

This is a question that many ask. They look at those with significant resources and assume that their generosity is minimal. If they were really generous, they would not have so much wealth, right?

For those of you who may be mulling over this thought, allow me to give you two thoughts.

First, the Bible does not indicate that wealth on its own is wrong. However, the Bible does tell us not to place our hope in wealth or be selfish with wealth.

When Paul writes to Timothy in 1 Timothy 6:17–19, he says this:

> *Instruct those who are rich in the present age not to be
> arrogant or to set their hope on the uncertainty of wealth,
> but on God, who richly provides us with all things to enjoy.
> Instruct them to do what is good, to be rich in good works,
> to be generous and willing to share, storing up treasure for
> themselves as a good foundation for the coming age, so that
> they may take hold of what is truly life.*

You see, money is always a heart issue, whether rich or poor.

Both those with much and those with little are to live appropriately.

Certainly, God is the giver of wealth. But He does not provide wealth for hoarding. He gives wealth to share. He gives wealth for generosity. He gives wealth to invest in eternal treasures. He gives wealth to advance His mission.

And here's the deal—you are probably the type of person Paul is writing about.

You are probably wealthy.

All of us are susceptible to comparison. We compare what we have with what others have. But those with whom we compare ourselves tend to be relatively few. And they also tend to be those who have more than we do.

This small, wealthier pool of individuals warps the way we view ourselves. We begin to think we are lacking in resources.

But are you?

There is a site called globalrichlist.com. This website allows you to type in your income or total wealth and compare it to those around the world. The results may surprise you.

Did you know that if someone makes $25,000 in a year, they are in the top 2 percent of the world? This means that 98 percent of the world's population makes less than $25,000.

You see, when Paul writes about the wealthy, he is not just writing about those you consider wealthy. It's not just the bosses at work, the business owners, and the families in that neighborhood across town.

He is likely writing about you.

So to you, and me—since *we* are the wealthy the Bible is talking about—let's get a realistic view on our possessions. Let's figure out how to live within our means. Let's look at how our lifestyle is affecting our ability to live the generous life. Let's seek God's guidance in how we use our wealth. And let's ask, "How much should we keep?"

Let's give generously.

Let's save wisely.

And let's live appropriately.

Are you up for the challenge?

———

Annie opened up the paper and read the challenges:

Day 15 Money Challenge: *Understand where you stand globally.* On the Internet, look up national GDP (Gross Domestic Product) rankings. It is a measure of national wealth. Pick out a country toward the bottom third. Spend some time learning about the people of that country and praying for them.

Day 16 Money Challenge: *Ask yourself the question, "How much should I keep?"* If you are married, this would be a great conversation topic with your spouse. Consider when enough will be enough for you.

Day 17 Money Challenge: *Look for an opportunity to help someone in need. Ask, "Is there anything I can do for you?"* And help them. Generous people do not wait for opportunities to come to them. They seek out ways to bless people.

CHAPTER 8

Used Cars Are Awesome

"Check this out." Annie set down a phone. "It's nice and cheap."

G.B. grinned big time. "I like it!"

"Living appropriately, right?" Annie jokily asked.

"It is a good start." G.B. grinned back at Annie. "If you want to give generously and save wisely, you must live appropriately. You can't spend more than you make and expect to accomplish either of those two goals."

Annie sat down in front of the desk. "So, where do people mess up the most?"

"Great question. It's usually either their home, car, food and entertainment, or education."

Annie simultaneously sighed and rolled her eyes. "I feel the education part."

G.B. responded in a comforting tone, "I know you do, Annie."

For the next thirty minutes, G.B. and Annie discussed some of the big decisions (both good and bad) people make that affect their ability to live appropriately. The entire time, Annie thought about how she too could live appropriately.

As their time came to an end, G.B. handed Annie her Money Challenges.

"Next time, I want to introduce you to the Joneses," G.B. stated.

"Okay. I look forward to meeting them," Annie replied agreeably.

"Oh, you already know them."

Annie suspiciously looked at G.B.

He just sat in his chair and smiled.

Should I Buy a House?

Unwise spending provides short-term enjoyment and long-term burdens. In the last chapter, we stated that living appropriately is managing your resources in a way that is both financially healthy and Kingdom-advancing.

The major spending areas that can derail appropriate living are our house, car, food and entertainment, and education. On their own, none of these are bad. But if we are not careful, we can find ourselves overextended for each of them.

Let's start with the house.

One of the big decisions you will face is whether or not to buy a house. For many, they perceive homeownership as a rite of passage into adulthood.

It is not.

It is a good decision for some, but not for others. Homeownership should only become a goal when it makes financial sense. How do you know when you are ready?

Let me give you three questions to which you must answer "yes" before purchasing a home.

I. Do you plan on living there for at least 5 years?

Any possible financial gain from owning a home can be destroyed in an early move. The purchase of a home comes with several upfront costs. Overcoming these costs takes time. Additionally, most of your mortgage payments are going toward interest in the early years.

Needless to say, there is not much gained in the first few years. The financial benefit of homeownership comes with time. If you are planning to move within five years, stick to renting.

2. Will your mortgage payments be less that 30 percent of your after-tax pay?

Do not place yourself in a position where you are "house poor," which means that all your money goes to pay the mortgage. Give your finances the flexibility that enables you to live a life of generosity. I recommend your mortgage should not be any greater than 30 percent of your after-tax pay. For example, if your after-tax pay is $6,000 per month, then your mortgage payment would be $1,800 ($6,000 x .30) or less.

3. Do you have at least 20 percent for a down payment?

If your mortgage is more than 80 percent of your home's value, you could get slapped with private mortgage insurance (PMI). This is an additional monthly fee lenders charge because you are considered a higher-risk borrower. PMI is to protect the lender not the borrower. That's right. They think the way you are borrowing is risky.

Take note. PMI costs you between .3 percent and 1.5 percent of your original loan balance every year. You will probably pay this until you have paid down 20 percent of your home's value and contacted the lender to have it removed. Don't be considered a risky borrower and put yourself in the position where you have to pay PMI.

If you can answer yes to these three questions, you might be ready for homeownership.

Also, don't forget to consider all the other costs associated with owning a home. Remember, this will be your home and you will be responsible for its upkeep. No more landlords to call when the hot water heater breaks and floods your house. You have to pay for it. Or when your kids clog the toilet and create a flood on the first-level floor, you pay for it. And, yes, I know about both of these expenses from experience.

Why You Buy a House

So that is the "When." But what about the "Why"? There are a few good reasons why you would buy a house, but the one that is most important often gets left out.

What is it?

To be free from a house payment down the road. *Homeownership is a long-term strategy to free up future cash flow.*

This is one of the most significant benefits to buying a home—putting yourself in a position to be free of a house payment one day.

We forget this all the time. Sometimes we don't focus on this benefit because it seems too far away and out of reach. And, sometimes, we act as if a mortgage payment is just an assumed part of life. We act as if it is something that will be with us until we die. Unfortunately, this mentality creates a self-fulfilling prophecy. We buy and make home-financing decisions that lead us down the path of a mortgage-for-lifer.

But this is not why you should buy a home. You also do not buy a home just to build equity and to have tax benefit. Those are good things, but they are not the end game. You buy a home to one day be free from a house payment. You buy a home to one day free up your future cash flow.

Take a moment and consider this:

What would your financial picture look like without a house payment?

How would your future retirement look different without a house payment?

What would your current and future generosity look like without a house payment?

Each one looks better without a monthly housing payment, right?

You should be thinking not just about owning a home, but about owning a home without debt. Realize that when you sign mortgage papers, you have not arrived. You have just started. And you should be thinking now, *How can I pay this thing off as quickly as possible?*

Homeownership is a long-term strategy.

Automobiles

Check this out—the average cost of a new car in 2013 was $32,252. As soon as you drove that car off the lot, the car's value depreciated by an average of 11 percent. Suddenly the car's value was $27,814. One year later, the average car had depreciated by 25 percent. And five years after the purchase of the new car, average depreciation was 63 percent. The car was worth only $11,629.[7]

Ouch.

Cars are depreciating assets. This means that, in most cases, a car will decrease in value over time. The money that you put into a car is almost sure to disappear.

The smell of a brand-new car is intoxicating. But that new car is one of the biggest wastes of money. As soon as you sign the papers and drive away, you lose a big chunk of money. Because of this, I am a big advocate of purchasing used cars. Let someone else take that initial hit.

The ability to get a quality used car has increased dramatically, especially at brand dealers or chain dealers. Many of the car dealers have implemented a rigid inspection standard to limit the risk of getting a bad car. Take advantage of this. Explore what the used lots have to offer before even considering sitting in a new car.

And when you purchase your used car, keep it as long as possible. Since a car goes down in value over time, you will almost never get what you paid for it. So if you are buying and selling a car every three years, you end up spending a significant amount of money on your automobile. Don't get swept up in the costly allure of having a new or newer car. Stretch out the life of your car.

Your budget will be glad you did.

Food and Entertainment

There was a time when I spent a lot of money on coffee. And I just drink black coffee. But a good cup of joe can cost a few dollars. And a few dollars every day, sometimes a few times in a single day, adds up.

Food and entertainment expenses fly under the radar in many people's financial picture. Many don't think about it because eating out has become a way of life.

How many times do you hear or ask, "Where do you want to go to eat?" The answer to this question is frequently more expensive than having a dinner date at home.

The weekend seems almost to mandate an entertainment expense. Movie? Concert? Sporting event? It's just what we do.

So how can you reduce these costs? Let's start with food.

Try taking your lunch to work. Eating out with your coworkers, especially if it isn't a lunch meeting, gets expensive.

Make a grocery-shopping list, and stick to it. It's tough enough not to purchase mint chocolate chip ice cream when you have a list. Walk through those grocery store doors without a list, and you are walking out with a pint of mint chocolate chip ice cream, guaranteed.

Limit leftovers by cooking appropriately sized meals. It seems easy to make too much food at home. It's just you and your spouse for dinner, but for some reason you are boiling an entire box of spaghetti. If you do have leftovers, save them for another meal.

Regarding entertainment, take full advantage of things that are free. In the city where I live, there are numerous free events throughout the year. Look on your city's website to see the upcoming free events in your area. You can check out your city's news sites as well. Of course, going outside is always free. When the weather is nice, go outside. Enjoy God's creation.

If you are accustomed to entertainment costing you something, take at least one weekend out of the year and take advantage of free options.

Having a fun weekend is good. Having a fun, free weekend is better.

College Education

Now let's talk education.

Education has quickly become one of the largest expenses you incur. This is due to the significant price hike in higher education over the years. Whether you, your spouse, or your kids are in college, you can take a big financial hit from college expenses.

You need to make it your mission to avoid student loan debt.

We have already discussed the need to save for college. It is the best plan to guard against student loan debt. But, eventually, the time to save ends and the time to spend begins. It will start with a simple, one-page acceptance letter that starts with "Congratulations!"

Graduating debt-free is not as easy as it was in the past, but it can be done. Every year, college graduates walk across a stage to receive their diplomas without any looming student loan debt payments.

And it starts before your child steps on campus.

Some of the most important financial decisions for college happen prior to college.

First, put more stock in your ability to learn well and work hard, not a diploma from a particular school. A forty- to fifty-year career is never determined by the name of a school on a diploma. If your child's "dream school" is expensive, help them gain a better perspective and be open to other schools.

Second, find a cost-effective option. Tuition prices do not determine education quality. There are many less expensive schools that are academically excellent. Find a school that balances a lower cost with good academics.

Third, check for available financial aid opportunities. This is not just governmental assistance. Most schools have several scholarship opportunities available. And some schools give tuition breaks.

Fourth, focus on the net cost. A $25,000/year school may provide your child with a 50-percent scholarship, but you are still paying $12,500 every year. A $10,000/year school with no financial assistance can actually be a wiser choice.

Fifth, if your child is in high school, encourage them to take courses that count toward college credit. These courses are typically cheap and will eliminate the need to take them at full cost in college.

Finally, encourage your child to do well in high school. This may open up more scholarship opportunities for them.

When your child is in college, they can help offset costs by finding an on-campus job that helps cover tuition, consistently checking with the financial aid office, and not taking classes that cannot be afforded. With the money you can spend, encourage them to take the largest class load they can handle. Those who stretch out their college education increase the likelihood of leaving school without a degree in hand.

Let's Wrap Up

Living appropriately is managing your resources in a way that is both financially healthy and Kingdom-advancing. So don't purchase a home unless you can put 20 percent down and have a payment that is less than 30 percent of your net income. Buy used cars. Watch your food and entertainment expenses. Limit eating out and take advantage of free entertainment. And avoid student loan debt by saving and exploring all options prior to the first day of class.

Now it is time for a few challenges.

———

Still curious about whom she was going to meet next time, Annie read her Money Challenges:

Day 18 Money Challenge: *Be generous with your home.* Invite your friends over for a meal. If you are tight on cash, do a potluck. Ask everyone to bring an entrée, side dish, or dessert.

Day 19 Money Challenge: *Plan a "free" weekend.* Figure out how to make it through the weekend without spending a single penny. For food, only use what you have in your home prior to Friday afternoon. Get creative and have fun!

Generosity Killers

CHAPTER 9

Generosity Killer #1—Keeping Up with the Joneses

"So where are they?" Annie questioned as she approached G.B.'s desk.

"Where are who?" G.B. replied.

"The Joneses? You told me that I was going to meet them today."

G.B. laughed. "The Joneses aren't real. It is just a way to identify those whose lifestyle you compare your lifestyle to."

Annie was a little disappointed and frustrated that she had not caught on earlier. "Keeping up with the Joneses. I get it now."

Annie sat down.

"Trying to maintain a similar lifestyle to those around you can be detrimental to your finances. What if you are comparing yourself to fakes?"

"Fakes?"

"Those who can't really afford the lifestyle they are living. They are constantly in debt and under financial strain."

Annie paused, then spoke. "You mean like me?"

"It's time to start appreciating the life you have, not desiring the life of someone else. More stuff won't make you happy, and you know it. Those who are generous appreciate and leverage the stuff they have."

G.B. gave her another folded piece of paper. He continued, "Focus on what you have, not what you don't have."

Annie took the paper from his hand.

Say Hello to the Joneses and Discontentment

The Joneses. You know them. You are probably familiar with the phrase "keeping up with the Joneses." It simply means to try to maintain the lifestyle that those around you have. The Joneses may be friends, family, neighbors, or coworkers. Their lifestyle pushes your lifestyle as you pace your standards, and consequently your purchases, with theirs.

Their perceived contentment pushes your discontentment.

And your chase to be like them causes you to make bad financial decisions while killing your ability to live openhandedly and generously.

Discontentment comes from a belief that our stuff is actually our stuff. We forget that we are simply managers of everything in our possession.

God is the owner. Not us.

The Bible tells us of an interaction between Jesus and a rich man (see Matt. 19:16–22). The rich man approached Jesus and asked Him what he must do to have eternal life. Jesus responded by telling him that he must follow several of the commands found in the Old Testament.

The rich man looked at Jesus and said that he had kept those commandments. He clearly thought highly of himself.

"What do I still lack?" the man questioned.

Jesus turned to him and answered that he must give all of his possessions away. With that, the rich man walked away sad. He could not let go of his stuff. He viewed his possessions as his possessions. And yet, he never really owned any of it. The owner was the one who stood before him. The owner was the one he had just turned his back on.

When we forget that the possessions under our watch are not actually our possessions, we find ourselves in a very dangerous place. We get attached, and we begin to base our lives on the car we drive, the house in which we live, and the vacations we get to take.

You see, chasing the Joneses is merely a symptom. Like a fever of someone who has the flu, discontentment is an indication of something more substantial.

Envy and jealousy of the Joneses occur when we center our lives on possessions. Because when our lives are centered on possessions, our primary hope for a better life is to have better possessions.

When we see that someone has something better than what we hold, we desire it because it represents a better life.

But you and I know that the money in our bank account and the car in our garage will not bring us fulfillment. This stuff will not give us a truly better life.

God designed us not to be hoarders, but to be conduits through which His generosity flows. Possessions were never meant to direct our lives. We were meant to direct our possessions. We were meant to use them for something so much larger than ourselves. We were meant to use them for a mission. We were meant to use them to show God's love to the world.

But this will not happen if we find ourselves affixed to the stuff that we are supposed to steward. Attachment and openhandedness cannot exist together. You must choose one or the other.

Which one will you choose?

The rich man missed eternity with his choice.

Just Your Average Joneses

The assumption that having the physical markings of wealth, like an expensive car, equates to financial health is dangerous.

To whom are you actually comparing yourself?

What if the Joneses were not who you thought they were? What if they had a secret identity that no one else knew but themselves? What if the house, the car, the clothes, the private school, were all a façade? What if your neighbors, who had all of the markings of a financially secure family, were not financially secure at all?

What if they were broke?

It is possible.

Americans are burdened with debt. The average U.S. household with debt has more than $15,000 in credit card debt. So if your neighbors have credit card debt, there is a possibility that they have a lot of it.[8]

What if you knew that your neighbor was living beyond their means, building up credit card balances to support a lifestyle they could not afford? Would your desire to have their lifestyle change?

It should.

Now, are all people with nice things broke and in debt? No. But some are.

And think about this: when you find yourself miserable because you want another person's lifestyle, it isn't just a symptom that indicates you may have the wrong perspective on possessions. You may also be comparing yourself to a façade instead of the real deal.

Finding Contentment

So how do we drive away discontentment? How do we get rid of looking to and wanting what the Joneses have? How do we stop thinking that the grass is actually greener on the other side?

Focus on What You Do Have

God has given everyone something. He has given you resources to manage. Compared to some, you may have less to manage. Compared to others, you may have more. But it is not about how much or how little you have.

When you find yourself dwelling on thoughts about the Joneses' car, house, or vacation, consider your own possessions. Appreciate what you do have. Think of five to ten reasons why you are thankful for your own car and house. And thank God for those blessings.

Next, consider how you take care of your current possessions. Do you treat what you have as disposable, as if you can afford to replace whatever God has given you, on a whim? Or are you treating your possessions as items entrusted to you by God?

Finally, spend time wondering how you can be generous with the resources you do have. Drown out the desire to live the Joneses' life by filling your mind with thoughts of gratefulness and stewardship.

None of us deserve anything we have been given. Once you realize that you are entitled to nothing, you will become grateful for everything. So let's concentrate on being thankful for and leveraging what we do have, and worry less about what we don't have.

Consider the Fate of Past Purchases

Peruse the items in your house. Are there some things that you haven't touched in a year? Or two years? Or three years? I have some items like that in my house.

I bet there was a time when you really desired that shirt or that old computer. But as time advanced, the desirability decreased. You moved on to other things.

Or what about the car that you once could not wait to drive? How do you feel about it now? It's amazing how a few coffee spills and several thousand miles on the odometer can make the appeal lessen.

Consider the fate of your past purchases. Maybe it will help you gain a better perspective on the allure of new purchases.

Reduce Your Social Media Snooping

When I post a picture on a social media site, like Facebook, I'm smiling. My kids and wife are smiling. It looks ideal. And I guess, in that moment, it is.

But what I don't post are the fights and the tears. They don't make it through the social media filter.

You do the same. We all do this.

Social media sites are a great way to connect and keep up with friends. But they are terrible at presenting reality.

If you hang out long enough on a social media site, you will begin to think that everyone else's life is perfect except yours. Everyone is always traveling, always remodeling their home, always eating gourmet meals, and always smiling.

But this is not reality.

Sometimes, it is best to take a break from social media. It allows you to get back into the real world and push aside the fictional, ideal story you are telling yourself about everyone else's lives.

Give Stuff Away

Want to stop being envious of the Joneses? Give stuff away. Generosity is an antidote for jealousy.

When you sense resource envy creeping into your heart, take a look around your house and see if there is anything you can give away. Remember those items you haven't touched in three years?

Try to start there. If you don't have any possessions to give away, give time. Find a way to serve at your local church or non-profit.

It is amazing how content you feel when you are giving stuff away. Because when you give away your possessions, you are forced to face reality—you already have more than enough.

Set Your Sights on Eternity

Earthly possessions are temporary. On the eternal time line, it seems ridiculous to obsess over a television that will be outdated in five years or over a car that will be full of rust and holes in a few decades.

Envy for our neighbors' toys demonstrates lack of eternal perspective. Set your sites on eternal treasures. Think about storing up for yourself treasures where neither moth nor rust destroys.

The Joneses are an ugly crew to chase. They can lead you down a road of financial hurt and scars. They are a generosity killer.

Stay away from them. Instead, consume yourself with trying to live with your hands wide open.

———

Annie peered at her next challenges:

Day 20 Money Challenge: *Be thankful and strategic.* Consider where you live and your primary mode of transportation. Write down five reasons you are thankful for each. Next, write down three ways you can leverage your residence and mode of transportation for God's mission.

Day 21 Money Challenge: *Give your stuff away.* Identify items you have not used for three years. Give or donate the items to an individual or organization that can use them.

Day 22 Money Challenge: *Speaking of the Joneses, introduce yourself to a neighbor whom you have not met.* Be sure to bring with you cookies or some type of small gift.

CHAPTER 10

Generosity Killer #2—Debt

"What are your credit cards' interest rates?"

Annie hated this question. She saw it every time a bill arrived in the mail.

"Anywhere between 15 percent and 24 percent. You don't have to tell me. It's terrible. I hate it."

"You know that your debt is destroying your ability to be generous and make an impact. Imagine if you could give away the money you are paying in interest alone."

Annie lightly closed her eyes for a few seconds. Debt had weighed on her mind for a while. She didn't like talking about it.

"I know. I could be a lot more generous."

"Sore spot? Okay. I won't berate you anymore. Let's talk about how to get rid of it instead."

Annie appreciated the positive shift in conversation. "Yes, let's do that instead."

In just a few minutes, G.B. explained how to systematically get rid of her debt. Annie felt encouraged and empowered. She thought it would be a lot more complicated that it was.

"Thank you for sharing that with me. I feel like I have a way out now," replied Annie.

"Paying off debt is not easy. It takes time. But it can be done. And being debt-free is worth the work. There is hope," G.B. said encouragingly. "Of course, this is for you."

G.B. passed on the next two Money Challenges to Annie.

"Thank you, G.B."

Our Big Debt Problem

Debt can be a terrible thing. It can put us in the position of always living on the verge of financial ruin. It can stress us out. And it can wreak havoc on our marriages.

Of course, debt is not your real issue. Debt is a symptom of a larger issue. It may be the result of trying to keep up with the Joneses. It may result from attempting to achieve life satisfaction through stuff. It may be the result of an addiction. Or it may simply be the result of a lack of discipline and planning. And more than likely, the consequences of this issue can be found in other areas beyond the bank account.

In the U.S., we really love our debt. At least, we make it seem like we do. Total U.S. household debt is in the trillions. Yes, you read that correctly—trillions. That is twelve zeroes.

Write that out and take a look at it.

We have $60 billion in credit card debt. Those who have credit card debt average a $15,000 balance.[9]

And we are getting pummeled by student loan debt. Those who just graduated college average $37,000 in student debt. Some 70 percent of 2016 college graduates had student loan debt.[10]

Consider this—let's say you have $30,000 in student loan debt. You average a 6 percent rate on your loans and have no fees. You want to get rid of the loans as soon as possible. So you consider a five-year repayment plan.

Over the next five years, your basic loan repayment plan would look like this:

Monthly payment: $579.98

Total interest paid: $4,799.08

Total amount paid: $34,799.08

If you think paying $4,799.08 in interest is a tough pill to swallow, try stretching the repayment plan to ten years. You end up paying $9,967.45 in interest.

Now what about credit cards? Credit cards are notorious for ridiculously high interest rates—10 percent, 20 percent, 30 percent.

Let's say you bought some furniture for $5,000. You didn't have the money, so you put it on your credit card with a 20 percent interest rate. You can only make the minimum monthly payment of $200. Guess what happens.

Over the next twelve years, you pay a total of $8,418 for your $5,000 purchase.

You better really like that sofa, loveseat, and ottoman.

For some of you, these examples are all too real. Some of you can relate to both the student loan debt and credit card debt examples. You've probably already done the math. In these two examples, you pay more than $13,000 just in interest.

The thought is painful.

Debt hinders our ability to move forward in our finances, and debt kills our generosity.

The Bible and Debt

The Bible talks about debt. In brief, here is what it says:

- Be cautious about going into debt.
- If you do go into debt, you will be burdened.
- Even though you hate the burden, you must still pay your bills.

The Bible warns us about the dangers of debt.

Proverbs 22:26–27 says, *"Don't be one of those who enter agreements, who put up security for loans. If you have nothing with which to pay, even your bed will be taken from under you."*

Simply put—be cautious about going into debt. Don't put yourself in the position where you struggle to make your payments. Carefully consider each purchase. If at all possible, avoid debt.

And the Bible tells us why.

Consider the words found in Proverbs 22:7—*"The rich rule over the poor, and the borrower is a slave to the lender."*

Anyone who has taken on debt understands how it feels to be a slave to the lender. You understand what it feels like to write a check or pay a bill online for a debt payment even when there are other ways you would like to use the money. You want to go on a vacation. You want to fix your car. You want to buy your children clothes for the new school year.

But you don't have a choice. The payment date arrives. And you pay the bill.

For some, the weight of debt is more significant than others. At times, you get frustrated. You get frustrated with paying interest. You get frustrated with a seemingly endless attachment to the debt. It is your ball and chain.

And if you choose not to pay, *even your bed will be taken from under you.* They can come after you. They can destroy your credit. They can repossess your stuff.

You are a slave to the lender.

Even though the weight of the debt is burdensome, you cannot shy away from your payment responsibilities. Psalm 37:21 says this—*"The wicked person borrows and does not repay, but the righteous one is gracious and giving."*

Wicked is a word that I do not want attached to my name. Not many would. But this is exactly how God describes those who avoid meeting their debt obligations. They are wicked.

There are consequences for our financial decisions. Some are good. Others are bad. The Bible makes it clear that the consequences for taking on too much debt are more the latter than the former.

Be cautious about going into debt.

If you do go into debt, you will be burdened.

And even though you have the burden, you must still pay your bills.

The Snowball Method

So how do you dig your way out of the mound of debt that covers you? How do you create light in your dark and seemingly grim financial picture?

Of all the different debt-free methods that are out there, my favorite is called the Snowball Method. People like Dave Ramsey and others champion this method.[11] And for good reason.

The concept is simple. Let debt balances determine the debt payoff sequence. Debts with lower balances are paid off before debts with higher balances. While focusing on one specific debt balance, make the minimum payment on all other debts.

Of course, remember these milestones before you start the snowball:

1. Start giving.
2. Save $1,500 for a minor emergency.
3. Max out your 401(k) or 403(b) match.

After you have done this, you are now ready to start the snowball. I am going to use some fictional numbers to demonstrate how the Snowball Method works.

Let's assume that you have four debts:

- $5,000 student loan with a 6% interest rate
- $7,500 car loan with an 8% interest rate
- $1,000 credit card balance with a 19% interest rate
- $300 credit card balance with a 15% interest rate

In this scenario, the order of debts to be paid off will be:

1. $300 credit card balance with a 15% interest rate
2. $1,000 credit card balance with an 19% interest rate
3. $5,000 student loan with a 6% interest rate
4. $7,500 car loan with an 8% interest rate

Like a snowball rolling down a hill, the idea behind the debt snowball method is momentum creation. There is excitement created by paying off a debt. This excitement develops a "can do" attitude that motivates debtors to eliminate the next debt balance. The excitement of paying off your $300 credit card will provide motivation to pay off the $1,000 credit card. Include all of your debts in the Snowball Method except your mortgage.

Debt is too much of a crushing force not to get rid of it. It ruins your ability to make the difference in this world that you were designed to make. Debt is a generosity killer.

So let's work to rid ourselves of this generosity killer. It's not easy. Sometimes, it can take a few years. But, the battle is worth the result—being debt-free and living the generous life.

Time for your next Money Challenges.

———————

As Annie looked at the paper, she read the following Money Challenges:

Day 23 Money Challenge: *Map out your debt-free plan.* Write down all of your debts. Using the Snowball Method, create a plan to pay off your debt. Mark down the order in which you will knock out those debts.

Day 24 Money Challenge: *Tell someone, "Thank you."* Identify someone who has been generous to you. Give them a call. Let them know what they mean to you and how truly grateful you are for them.

Generosity Killer #3—Disorganization

Annie took her usual seat in front of G.B.'s desk.

"The coolest thing happened to me yesterday," Annie started.

"Tell me about it," replied G.B.

"So I had just finished my Money Challenge, calling someone from my past that I needed to thank, and I received a phone call. It was a former acquaintance named Mary. I had completely forgotten about her. We lived in the same dorm my freshman year of college. She simply called to thank me for being there for her when her boyfriend broke up with her. I barely remembered it."

"Well, it clearly made a difference in her life."

"It really did. Apparently, whatever I said helped her move on. Within a few months she met her future husband. They are now happily married and living here in Chicago."

"That's a great story, Annie. By being generous with your time, you helped change Mary's life."

"It really meant a lot for me to hear from her." Annie clasped her hands together. "Now, what do I need to do today?"

"Start a budget."

Annie gave G.B. an unimpressed expression. "Yuck."

"If you are going to accomplish a goal, you need a plan. Your budget is your plan."

"Seems like work."

"It's not that bad. Just set aside a few hours for dreaming and scheming. You'll have a basic budget completed in no time. You do want to be a part of something bigger, living with open hands, right?"

"I do."

"Well, you need a plan."

G.B. started jotting notes on his notepad. He showed Annie a simple way to put together a budget. Annie began to realize she could do this. It wasn't as scary as she thought. And she liked the thought of knowing exactly where her money went. She felt like she could have more control over it.

"Okay. I think I can do it," Annie said with some certainty.

"Of course you can. Here are your Money Challenges."

G.B. slid the folded paper containing the challenges across the desk.

He continued, "And next time you hear from Mary, tell her I said, 'hello.'"

Annie looked at G.B., her eyebrows ruffled with confusion. G.B. just winked back at her.

"Sure," said Annie with a puzzled voice.

The Danger of Disorganization (Why You Need a Budget)

Desire is good.

Intention is good.

Motivation is good.

But you can have the greatest of desires, the strongest of intentions, and the deepest of motivations, and without organization, change will be difficult.

Even though you know it's needed, you hate hearing about it. In fact, there is a single word that brings shivers down the spine of many. You know what I am about to say—*budget.*

There, it has been said.

For most, budgets mean work. It means complexity. It means restrictions. If you could describe how you feel about budgeting, you would describe it in this way—blah.

And I get that response. But is it the right response?

You see, a budget is just a plan. That's it.

You plan all the time. You plan your weekly and monthly schedule. You plan your vacation. You even plan what you will watch on television.

And why do you plan? Because you want to accomplish something.

I like sports. As a University of Kentucky graduate, I enjoy watching the Kentucky Wildcats play. And every time I watch a game, the television announcers inevitably discuss the team's game plan. What defense will they play? What offense will they run?

Why is a game plan so important? Because they want to win. No team would ever start a game without a plan to win.

If you want to right your financial picture so that you can live generously, you need a plan to succeed. A budget does this for you.

A budget helps you spend less than you earn, and makes sure that the money you have goes toward areas of importance, not waste. It puts you on the path to success.

Disorganization hinders generosity. It is a generosity killer.

Organization accelerates generosity.

So let's start a budget.

Here are a few steps to get you going.

Starting a Budget

Step 1: Determine your monthly goals.

I like monthly budgets. Given income and bill cycles, they make the most sense.

The first step to a monthly budget is determining your goals. Before you start your budget, you should at least have some giving and saving goals in mind.

These goals will shape your budget as you move forward.

You might not be able to set aside 15 percent for retirement in the first month, but you may be able to do something.

You may not be able to give 10 percent right away, but you may need to include your 1 percent, the start of your Takeoff.

As you consider your budget, consider your goals. Your budget is your plan to reach them.

Step 2: Determine your typical monthly income.

The next step in creating your monthly budget is to figure out how much you get paid on a monthly basis. For some, this may be easy. You simply look at your paycheck. Those whose pay varies may need to use their average monthly income. If you happen to know in which months you get paid more than others, adjust your monthly budget accordingly.

For most of you, it is your net income that hits your account. Taxes are already taken out for you. If you fit into this category, consider your net income while budgeting.

If taxes are not taken out, you will use your gross pay, but you will need to remember taxes in the next step.

Step 3: Determine your typical monthly expenditure.

Make a list. Go back and take a look at your past month's expenses. These will be the starting point for budgeting your expenses.

Consider whether or not you can group the expenses into categories. Common categories include giving, retirement, mortgage/rent, groceries, transportation, insurance, medical, education, and entertainment. You may identify a few more. If you used your gross income in Step 1, be sure to include taxes as a category.

Don't overdo the categories. Excessive categories will make the budget appear cumbersome and complex. An effective budget is often a simple budget.

Step 4: Adjust your expenditures to fit your income (and your ability to give and save).

Once you have categorized each expenditure, determine whether or not the total is less than your income. If your spending is greater than your income, you have some work to do.

Spending more than you make is a recipe for financial difficulties.

Find areas that you can pull back on. Many of these may be lifestyle expenditures. You may need to reduce how much you eat out. You may need to consider getting a less expensive, preferably debt-free, car.

Some of these decisions are going to be easier than others. But you must live within your means.

Of course, there may be some areas that you need to increase— giving and saving. You may need to increase the amount you can put toward existing debts. If you cannot *give generously* and *save wisely*, let your budget help you uncover why.

Let your budget help you reach your goals.

Step 5: Track your spending.

Once you have completed your budget, begin to track your spending. You need to ensure that you do not overspend.

There are several ways to track spending. Some use the "enve-lope system." This is where you place cash into an envelope at the beginning of each month that represents each category of your budget. You might have a "groceries" envelope, or a "eating out" envelope, or an "entertainment" envelope. Once the cash in the envelope runs out, you don't spend anymore. The envelope system pushes you to be disciplined and thoughtful with your spending.

If you don't want to carry around a bunch of cash everywhere, consider one of the many online options. I like Mint.com. It seems to work well by tracking your online banking data into a visual dashboard. But there are several other great online platforms out there as well.

Find one that fits you.

Step 6: Have a monthly check-in.

At the end of each month, check to see how you did. Did you overspend in some areas? Did you underspend in some areas? Did you save enough? Where you free to be generous?

Review the budget to determine if you need to make any adjustments. Consider the upcoming month. Are there expenses that will hit next month that did not hit last month, like insurance? Be sure to include these in next month's budget.

The great thing about monthly budgets is that you get to start fresh twelve times a year.

Hello, Organization

Disorganization is a generosity killer. A budget is a great tool to get you back on track financially.

A budget does not have to be an overwhelming, complex beast that you must endure. It is your game plan. It is your plan for success.

You are not budgeting to restrict yourself; you are budgeting to free yourself. You are budgeting to remove the shackles left by poor financial decision-making.

Those shackles will fall off. But their disappearance will not be by accident. It will result from you being purposeful.

It will result from you having a plan.

It will result from you having a budget.

Say good-bye to disorganization, and say hello to organization. And now say hello to your next Money Challenges.

————

As Annie walked through the bank's front lobby, she glanced down at her next challenges:

Day 25 Money Challenge: *Create a budget.* Do some dreaming and scheming. Figure out what areas you can reduce or cut to align with the "Give Generously, Save Wisely, Live Appropriately" formula.

Day 26 Money Challenge: *Identify something you can do for others for free.* Then, offer it to someone. Maybe it's babysitting. Maybe it's mowing the lawn. Maybe it's providing consulting in your area of expertise. Be generous with your time and your talent.

CHAPTER 12

Generosity Killer #4—The Financially Separate Marriage

When Annie walked back into the bank, she was shocked and overjoyed. There at G.B.'s desk was Mary, the lady she knew from her freshman year of college. Annie briskly walked over to Mary and gave her a hug.

"It is so good to see you! Thank you for your call! And what are you doing here?" Annie was giddy.

G.B. interjected. "Mary and her husband are here because I wanted you to learn how to have a financially healthy marriage. I know you are not married yet, but you might be one day."

"Your husband is here? That's great!" exclaimed Annie. Because of the phone call from Mary, she felt a special connection to their marriage.

"Here he is," Mary said as she pointed at a man walking across the bank toward them. "Annie meet Terry. Terry meet Annie."

Annie was shocked. She remembered Terry. Terry was the one who spoke to her when she walked into the bank for the very first time. He was the one who introduced her to G.B.

"We've met before. Here, in the bank, right? And we've talked on the phone," questioned Terry.

Annie curiously looked at Terry. "Phone?"

G.B. spoke, "Terry is the owner of Terry's Auto Shop. I believe you had some car work done there."

For a second, Annie did not know what to say. So she said the first thing that came to mind.

"Thank you."

"No need to thank me. We've all been there. G.B. helped change everything for me. The least I could do was be generous to someone whose shoes I've been in."

Annie put the pieces together. "You did the Money Challenges. That is why you asked me in the bank if you could do anything for me! And, Mary, that is why you called me!"

Mary smiled and said, "We did them a while back. Now we don't need a folded sheet of paper telling us what to do. It's just how we try to live—generously."

G.B. interjected, "Well, I want you all to catch up. But first, Terry and Mary, why don't you tell Annie about what you've learned about money and marriage."

"Happy to," replied Terry. "And, man, I wish I was like you, Annie, learning this stuff before marriage. Many heated arguments could have been avoided."

Annie sat and listened to Terry and Mary tell their story and the lessons learned from it. It gave Annie a better understanding of what she needed to do if she ever got married.

At the end of their time, Annie hugged Terry and Mary. She felt like she had discovered two new, great friends.

As Annie walked away she heard G.B.'s voice, "Don't forget this."

It was her next challenges.

Annie turned around and took the paper from G.B.'s hand and said, "Thank you for everything."

What's with All This Fighting?

A lack of financial unity in a marriage often leads to a lack of generosity. The disjointed nature of finances makes it difficult to determine when to give and to whom you should give. Financially separate marriages present risks to a couple's financial picture, generosity, and their marriage.

One of the greatest causes of marital disagreements is money. A study by Fidelity Investments revealed that 51 percent of couples admitted to arguing either frequently or occasionally about their finances.[12] You probably can relate.

We all enter into our marriages with different financial personalities. Some of us are spenders. Others are savers. More than likely, your financial personality differs from your spouse.

We also come from different financial backgrounds. Some of us come from families that demonstrated great financial discipline.

Others came from financially broken households. Some grew up talking about money. For others, money was a scary, taboo subject.

Opposites attract, right?

Opposites also create tension.

Perhaps you grew up with little and your spouse grew up with plenty. Therefore, you tend to be more cautious with money than your spouse. You think through your purchases as if it is the only purchase you will make in your lifetime. Your spouse holds the world record for "Fastest Credit Card Swipe."

And the tension continues to build.

Different financial personalities can also lead to different financial goals. Maybe you would like to pay for your kids' college while your spouse would like to pay off the mortgage. You cannot do both. Money is a finite resource. You have to choose between competing preferences. The lack of consensus can create stress anytime the tuition or mortgage payment is due.

And the tension continues to build.

When financial trouble hits, our disjointedness creates arguments. You realize that you are not on the same page as your spouse. And you battle about it.

You try to argue your point while your spouse's financial personality, history, and goals push her or him to argue for a completely different point.

And it is miserable.

You must get on the same financial page.

Getting on the Same Financial Page

Financial matters do not have to bring division in a marriage. They can actually serve as a point of unification. So if we know that getting on the same financial page is important, how do we do it?

Let me suggest eight steps to bring about unification:

1. *Agree that you need to agree.* This seems simple enough, but many couples operate as if it is not important. He has his goals. She has her goals. Getting on the same financial page starts by acknowledging the need for unification.

2. *Replace "mine" with "ours."* The way in which you communicate ownership of your and your spouse's money is telling. When talking about money, use "our" instead of "mine." "My money" is exclusive and promotes individualism. "Our money" is inclusive and promotes cooperation.

3. *Take a look at reality.* What does your cash flow really look like? What is your real wealth? How far are you *really* from retiring? How much do you *really* owe? One of the greatest mistakes you can make is to assume you are financially better off than you really are. This assumption leads to poor financial decisions. Uncovering reality may not be fun, but it is necessary.

4. *Dream together.* After determining where you are, determine where you want to go. I recommend doing this in five-year increments. What do you want your future to look like? You will probably have different dreams. Be willing to do a little compromising and create an envisioned future you can both chase.

5. *Develop dream-reaching goals.* Once you have agreed what
    the dream looks like, figure out what goals must be reached
    to get there. How quickly can debt be paid off? How much
    must be saved? How much do you need in retirement?

6. *Identify goal-reaching milestones.* It can become wearisome
    to chase a five- or ten-year goal. Identify milestones along
    the way to celebrate. Paying off a credit card balance,
    downsizing your home, or hitting your emergency savings
    goal can all be great milestones.

7. *Every year ask, "What do we need to accomplish this year?"*
    As you look at your milestones, figure out what must be
    done each year. Set priorities for the year. This can greatly
    reduce conflict over how money is used throughout the
    years.

8. *Continue learning together.* We are all destined to be wid-
    ows and widowers. At some point, one of you will be forced
    to manage the finances alone. Make sure both of you are
    prepared to do so.

If you are both on the same financial page with yearly priorities
that help you get to a shared dream, you have made a huge step to
reaching that dream.

And a huge step toward reducing arguments over money.

Get Joint Accounts

At my former church, I had the opportunity to spend time
with those in our premarital class and discuss money. One of the

very first pieces of advice I would give them was to, once married, get joint accounts. Avoid accounts that your spouse cannot access.

The reason is simple—marriage is an all-in deal. You get all of your spouse and they get all of you. This includes your bank account.

Joint accounts communicate "our money." In a marriage, the statement "Well, it's my money so . . ." is a lie and is divisive. Joint accounts tell your spouse the money you or your spouse makes is just as much theirs as it is yours. It does not matter who makes more or less money for the family. It is both the husband's and the wife's money—every single penny.

Joint accounts also communicate "our expenditures." Whether hidden or in plain sight, your purchases affect your spouse. If you have poor purchase habits, your spouse feels the fallout. Married couples do not make financial decisions in a vacuum. Joint accounts encourage input from both spouses in determining expenditures.

Joint accounts communicate transparency. When both have access to the accounts, there is no hiding of purchases. It tells your spouse you want them to be aware of your purchases—that there is nothing you are hiding from them.

Joint accounts communicate trust. Accounts to which both husband and wife have access demonstrate a belief that the spouse will handle money in an agreed-upon way.

Each has confidence in the other.

So what do separate accounts communicate? Unlike joint accounts, separate accounts can communicate a desire to remain free of accountability and responsibility to one another. Separate accounts communicate you are not ready to bring everything into the marriage and can also communicate you want to maintain a way out.

Pooling finances raises the level of accountability and responsibility. And it demonstrates that you are committed to your spouse.

Every part of you is theirs, including the bank account.

In marriage, it is not "my money" and "my expenditures" but "our money" and "our expenditures."

Strive for marriage that has financial unity. Do this for the sake of generosity. Do this for the sake of your marriage.

———

Smiling as Annie walked away from G.B., she looked at her challenges:

Day 27 Money Challenge: *Get to know your financial personality.* Are you a spender, saver, planner, avoider, or other? Write down some characteristics that you feel define your financial personality. Write the strengths and weaknesses of each characteristic. If you are married, have a discussion about them with your spouse at a coffee shop. Try to keep the conversation light-hearted.

Day 28 Money Challenge: *Give your spouse access to all of your accounts.* Sometimes this may mean adding them to the account. Other times, this may simply mean giving them the username and password for online access. Make each account "our" account, not "my" account.

CHAPTER 13

Your Path to Living Generously

It had been a great ride for Annie. While she had not solved all of her financial woes yet, she had hope. She knew that she could do it. She knew that she could align herself with God's design for her and her money.

"You have work to do, Annie, but you are on the right track. I have a feeling that things are going to be different for you moving forward," responded G.B.

Annie inquisitively looked at G.B. "How do you do all of this? I mean, how do you make such a difference in so many people's lives? And now they are making a difference too. What's the secret?"

"There's no secret, Annie. I just live generously and let God take care of the rest."

"G.B., the Generous Banker."

"It's really George Bailey. At least, that's what my birth certificate says." G.B. had a huge grin across his face.

"Your last Money Challenge," he said, as he handed her a piece of paper.

Annie smiled back and began to turn toward the bank's door. But as she did, what she saw stopped her in her tracks.

It was the man who ran into her a few weeks ago. Annie thought to herself, *What is he doing here?*

A Path to Living Generously

We discussed how to *give generously, save wisely,* and *live appropriately.* But you may find yourself asking, "So what do I need to do first, second, third, etc.?" This is a common and good question.

You need a path. A milestone is an important marker on a journey. It is a point of celebration. So let's look at eight important milestones on your path to living generously.

Milestone I: Start giving.

God designed giving to be our first financial priority. Some of you may already give. Keep it up. Some need to start. Use The Takeoff plan if necessary. Make sure your local church is the primary focus of your giving.

Milestone 2: Save $1,500 for a minor emergency.

Assuming that you are giving away a percentage of your gross income, start saving. Set aside enough for a minor emergency. A great goal is $1,500.

Milestone 3: Max out your 401(k) or 403(b) match.

If your employer offers a contribution match, take it. Do not miss out on this incredible return on your money. Max out your match, but do not go beyond it.

Milestone 4: Pay off all debt except your mortgage.

Now it's time to pay off your debt. Get rid of those high interest rate payments. Use the Snowball Method—pay off your smallest debt balances first.

Milestone 5: Save 3–6 months of living expenses for a job-loss emergency.

Now that you are debt-free (except your mortgage), boost your emergency savings. Be sure to calculate the amount based on your financial responsibility for others.

Milestone 6: Put 15 percent of your gross income to retirement.

Ramp up your retirement contributions. If you are approaching retirement, check out a retirement calculator to see if you need to do more than 15 percent.

Milestone 7: Save for college or pay off your mortgage.

Both are good options. If you have kids, I recommend the former first.

Place money into an investment account, like a 529 Plan. Make sure you research your plan. There are plans that do better than others.

Getting rid of your mortgage may take some time, but it is worth it. Remember, the main reason you purchased a house is to eventually be free of a monthly payment. Home ownership is a long-term strategy to free up future cash flow.

Milestone 8: Live generously.

As your financial health has strengthened, so has your generosity.

Now it's time to take your generosity to a whole new level. Live more openhandedly than you ever have before. Make a difference in the lives of those around you. Make a difference for the sake of Kingdom advancement. Make an impact for all eternity.

God did not design us to be hoarders, but conduits through which His generosity flows. Putting yourself in a position where you can live generously is not always easy. But these steps will help you get there. They will help you get to a place where your concern is not about which credit card payment to make, but which person or organization you can help.

––––––––

Annie quickly looked down at her final Money Challenges. She read the first one. Annie couldn't help but smirk and lightly shake her head.

Day 29 Money Challenge: *Help someone who, in your opinion, doesn't deserve it.* And it doesn't have to be financial help. Try to identify a need they have and help them with it. If you can't spot a need, write them an encouraging note.

CHAPTER 14

One Last Challenge

Annie stared at him.

It was the man who had run over her a few weeks ago.

But he was not as she remembered. Something was different. He looked stressed, disheveled, and desperate. The arrogance she remembered seemed to have been stripped from him.

And in a twist that surprised Annie, she found herself feeling bad for him. Maybe it was because she remembered that not too long ago, she was the one walking through those doors in a desperate search for something, anything.

Maybe it had something to do with the final challenge that she held in her hand, but she wondered what it looked like to live generously in this moment. Annie felt compelled to go over to him.

So she thanked G.B. again, put her challenges in her purse, and walked over to him.

The beauty of this moment God had provided Annie was not lost on her. She remembered the Money Challenge question that Terry had asked her in this very spot: "Is there anything that I can do for you?"

"I really don't know. I just feel lost."

"My name is Annie." She reached out her hand.

"Charles." He reciprocated. Annie was now shaking hands with the man who had bowled her over.

Charles continued, "My life is a mess. I thought I was doing well. I had a good-paying job. I had nice things. But I got laid off." He paused.

"This is embarrassing. I don't even know you. Even though I made good money, I still lived beyond my means. I was living a lie. And now, I have debt, no job, and no idea what to do. To top things off, I sacrificed my family for it all. I was a bad husband and dad. And for what?"

He paused again and repeated himself.

"For what?"

Charles let out a large sigh, hung his head, and said, "There just has to be more than this."

He was hurting. And though Annie wanted to bring up the incident that had happened, she didn't. She wasn't going to mess up this God-given moment. Instead, she did something that would have shocked her only a few weeks ago.

She helped.

"You see that man over there?" Annie pointed at G.B.

"Yes."

"You should talk to him. People call him G.B. I believe it actually stands for George Bailey, but everyone likes to say that it stands for Generous Banker."

"That's weird."

"Trust me, I know. But you need to meet with him."

Annie waved at G.B. He waved back.

"Go over there and talk to him," Annie said as she patted his back twice.

As Annie watched Charles walk toward G.B., she turned to walk out the door. Annie knew she had done the right thing.

The Chicago wind hit Annie as she stepped onto the sidewalk. Cars busily rolled by on the street, their honking horns echoing off the large buildings.

In the midst of the city noise, a voice called out to her, "Excuse me, ma'am. Do you have any change?"

Annie recognized the voice. It was Randall. He was standing there smiling, just like she remembered him doing before. But before she could smile back, a brief moment of despair hit her. How could she help? Then, she remembered something.

Annie reached into her purse and pulled out her wallet. When she had returned her super expensive phone and bought the cheaper phone, the cashier had given her the cost difference in cash. As she opened up her wallet, there it was.

"Sure thing, Randall," she said, as she handed him a ten-dollar bill.

Even with those three missing teeth, he had the most contagious grin. Just like when she first met Randall, Annie gave him a hug. And again, Randall hugged back.

"Thank you, miss. I bet you are going to be a part of something big in this world."

As Annie released her hug, she looked straight into Randall's eyes. "I already am."

Before she started to walk away, she remembered that there was one last challenge on the paper.

Annie pulled the piece of paper out of her purse and read her last challenge:

Day 30 Money Challenge: *Living generously is not just about money. Live openhandedly with every resource God has given you. Always remember, God designed us not to be hoarders, but conduits through which His generosity flows.*

Annie was ready.
Are you?

Notes

1. L. B. Aknin, J. K. Hamlin, and E. W. Dunn, "Giving Leads to Happiness in Young Children," *PLOS ONE 7*, no. 6 (2012): e39211.

2. E. W. Dunn, L. B. Aknin, and M. I. Norton, "Prosocial Spending and Happiness Using Money to Benefit Others Pays Off," *Current Directions in Psychological Science* 23, no. 1 (2014): 41–47.

3. Randy Alcorn, *The Treasure Principle: Unlocking the Secret of Joyful Giving* (Colorado Springs, CO: Multnomah Books, 2001), 41.

4. Report on the Economic Well-Being of U.S. Households in 2015; https://www.federalreserve.gov/2015-report-economic-well-being-us-households-201605.pdf.

5. Marsha L. Richins, "When Wanting Is Better than Having: Materialism, Transformation Expectations, and Product-Evoked Emotions in the Purchase Process," *Journal of Consumer Research* 40, no. 1 (2013): 1–18.

6. John Cortines and Gregory Baumer, *God and Money: How We Discovered True Riches at Harvard Business School* (Carson, CA: Rose Publishing, 2016).

7. See https://www.trustedchoice.com/insurance-articles/wheels-wings-motors/car-depreciation/.

8. See https://www.nerdwallet.com/blog/credit-card-data/average-credit-card-debt-household/.

9. Ibid.

10. See http://blogs.wsj.com/economics/2016/05/02/student-debt-is-about-to-set-another-record-but-the-picture-isnt-all-bad/?mod=e2tw#:Xhy9NQQoFnzvDA.

11. Dave Ramsey, *The Total Money Makeover: Classic Edition: A Proven Plan for Financial Fitness* (Nashville, TN: Nelson Books, 2013).

12. "This Valentine's Day, Say 'I Do' to Putting Your Financial House in Order," *Fidelity Investments* (February 5, 2014). Retrieved from https://www.fidelity.com/about-fidelity/individual-investing/this-valentines-day-say.